Junior High Talksheets

Psalms and Proverbs

D1378911

YOUTH SPECIALTIES TITLES

Professional Resources
Advanced Peer Counseling in Youth Groups
The Church and the American Teenager
    (previously released as Growing Up in America)
Developing Spiritual Growth in Junior High Students
Feeding Your Forgotten Soul
Help! I'm a Volunteer Youth Worker!
High School Ministry
How to Recruit and Train Volunteer Youth Workers
    (previously released as Unsung Heroes)
Junior High Ministry (Revised Edition)
The Ministry of Nurture
Organizing Your Youth Ministry
Peer Counseling in Youth Groups
The Youth Minister's Survival Guide
Youth Ministry Nuts and Bolts

Discussion Starter Resources
Amazing Tension Getters
Get 'Em Talking
High School TalkSheets
Junior High TalkSheets
More High School TalkSheets
More Junior High TalkSheets
Option Plays
Parent Ministry TalkSheets
Tension Getters
Tension Getters Two
To Do or Not To Do

Ideas Library
Ideas Combo 1-4, 5-8, 9-12, 13-16, 17-20,
21-24, 25-28, 29-32, 33-36, 37-40, 41-44,
45-48, 49-52, 53, 54
Ideas Index 1-52

Youth Ministry Programming
Adventure Games
Creative Bible Lessons
Creative Programming Ideas for Junior High Ministry
Creative Socials and Special Events
Good Clean Fun
Good Clean Fun, Volume 2
Great Fundraising Ideas for Youth Groups
Great Games for City Kids
Great Ideas for Small Youth Groups
Greatest Skits on Earth
Greatest Skits on Earth, Volume 2
Holiday Ideas for Youth Groups (Revised Edition)
Hot Illustrations for Youth Talks
Hot Talks
Junior High Game Nights
More Junior High Game Nights
On-Site: 40 On-Location Youth Programs
Play It! Great Games for Groups

Play It Again! More Great Games for Groups
Road Trip
Rock Talk
Super Sketches for Youth Ministry
Teaching the Bible Creatively
Teaching the Truth About Sex
Up Close and Personal: How to Build Community in
    Your Youth Group

4th-6th Grade Ministry
Attention Grabbers for 4th-6th Graders
4th-6th Grade TalkSheets
Great Games for 4th-6th Graders
How to Survive Middle School
Incredible Stories
More Attention Grabbers for 4th-6th Graders
More Great Games for 4th-6th Graders
Quick and Easy Activities for 4th-6th Graders
More Quick and Easy Activities for 4th-6th Graders
Teach 'Toons

Clip Art
ArtSource Volume 1—Fantastic Activites
ArtSource Volume 2—Borders, Symbols, Holidays and
    Attention Getters
ArtSource Volume 3—Sports
ArtSource Volume 4—Phrases and Verses
ArtSource Volume 5—Amazing Oddities and
    Appalling Images
ArtSource Volume 6—Spiritual Topics
Youth Specialties Clip Art Book
Youth Specialties Clip Art Book, Volume 2

Video
Edge TV
God Views
Next Time I Fall in Love Video Curriculum
Promo Spots for Junior High Game Nights
Understanding Your Teenage Video Curriculum
Witnesses

Student Books
Going the Distance
Good Advice
Grow for It Journal
Grow for It Through the Scriptures
How to Live with Your Parents Without Losing
    Your Mind
I Don't Remember Dropping the Skunk, But I
    Do Remember Trying to Breathe
Next Time I Fall in Love
Next Time I Fall in Love Journal

Junior High Talksheets

Psalms and Proverbs

50 Discussion Starters
from the Scriptures

Rick Bundschuh
and Tom Finley

Youth Specialties

ZondervanPublishingHouse

Grand Rapids, Michigan
A Division of HarperCollins Publishers

Junior High TalkSheets Psalms and Proverbs

Copyright ©1994 by Youth Specialties, Inc.

Youth Specialties Books, 1224 Greenfield Drive, El Cajon, California 92021, are published by Zondervan Publishing House, 5300 Patterson, S.E., Grand Rapids, Michigan 49530.

Library of Congress Cataloging-in-Publication Data

Bundschuh, Rick, 1951-
    Junior high talksheets : Psalms and Proverbs : 50 discussion starters
    from Scripture / Rick Bundschuh and Tom Finley.
        p.   cm.
    ISBN 0-310-49141-X : $12.95
    1. Bible. O.T. Psalms—Study. 2. Bible. O.T. Proverbs—Study. 3. Junior high school students—Religious life.
4. Church group work with teenagers. I. Finley, Tom, 1951- . II. Title. III. Title: Junior high talk sheets.
BS1451.B86 1994
268'.433—dc20

                                                                    94-16425
                                                                    CIP

Edited by Noel Bechetti and Lorraine Triggs
Cover and interior designed by Church Art Works

Printed in the United States of America

94 95 96 97 98 99/ML/6 5 4 3 2 1

Table of Contents

HOW TO USE TALKSHEETS

You have in your possession a very valuable book. It contains fifty instant discussions for junior high youth groups. Inside, you will find reproducible TalkSheets covering a wide variety of hot topics, plus simple step-by-step instructions on how to use them. All you need for fifty thought-provoking meetings is this book and access to a copy machine.

TalkSheets are versatile and easy to use. They can be utilized in a group meeting, a Sunday school class, or during Bible study. They can be used either in small or large groups of people. The discussions they instigate can be as brief as twenty minutes, or as long as interest remains and time allows. You can build an entire youth group meeting around a single TalkSheet, or you can use TalkSheets to supplement other materials and resources you might be using. The possibilities are endless.

TalkSheets are much more than just another type of curriculum or workbook. They invite excitement and involvement in discussing important issues and growth in faith. TalkSheets deal with key topics that young people want to talk about. With interesting activities, challenging questions, and eye-catching graphics, TalkSheets will capture the attention of your audience and will help them think and learn. The more you use TalkSheets, the more your young people will look forward to them.

TALKSHEETS ARE DISCUSSION STARTERS

While TalkSheets can be used as curriculum for your program, they are primarily designed to be used as discussion starters. Everyone knows the value of a good discussion in which young people are interacting with each other. When they are talking about a given subject, they are most likely thinking seriously about it and trying to understand it better. They are formulating and defending their points of view and making decisions and choices. Discussion helps truth rise to the surface, thereby making it easier for young people to discover it for themselves. There is no better way to encourage learning than through discussion.

A common fear among youth group leaders reticent about leading a group of young people in discussion is, "What if the kids in my group just sit there and refuse to participate?" It is because of this fear that many choose to show a movie or give a prepared lecture.

Usually, the reason young people fail to take part in a discussion is simple: They haven't had the time or the opportunity to organize their thoughts. Most junior high students haven't yet developed the ability to "think on their feet"—to be able to present their ideas spontaneously and with confidence. They are afraid to speak for fear they might sound stupid.

TalkSheets remove this fear. They offer a chance to interact with the subject matter in an interesting, challenging, and nonthreatening way, *before* the actual discussion begins. Not only does this give them time to organize their thoughts and to write them down, but it also helps remove any anxiety they might feel. Most will actually look forward to sharing their answers and hearing others' responses to the same questions. They will be ready for a lively discussion.

A STEP-BY-STEP USER'S GUIDE

TalkSheets are very easy to use, but do require some preparation on your part. Follow these simple instructions and your TalkSheet discussion will be successful:

1 **Choose the right TalkSheet for your group.** Each TalkSheet deals with a different topic. The one you choose will have a lot to do with the needs and the maturity level of your group. It is not necessary (or recommended) to use the TalkSheets in the order in which they appear in this book.

2 **Try it yourself.** Once you have chosen a specific TalkSheet, answer the questions and do the activities yourself. Imagine your students participating. This "role playing" will give you firsthand knowledge of what you will be requiring of your young people. As you fill out the TalkSheet, think of additional questions, activities, and Scriptures.

3 **Read the Leader's Instructions on the back of each TalkSheet.** Numerous tips and ideas for getting the most out of your discussion are contained in the Leader's Instructions. Add your own thoughts and ideas. Fill in the date and the name of the group in the top right hand corner of the leader's page.

4 **Remove the TalkSheet from the book.** The information is easier to copy when removed. Before making copies, you might wish to "white out" (with liquid paper) the page number.

5 **Make enough copies for everyone.** Each student will need his or her own copy. This book makes the assumption that everyone has access to a copy machine but any method of duplicating will suffice. Only the student's side of the TalkSheet needs to be copied. The leader's material on the other side is just for you, the leader. Keep in mind that you are able to make copies for your group because we have given you permission to do so. U.S. copyright laws haven't changed. It is still mandatory that you request permission from a publisher before making copies of other published material. It is illegal not to do so. Permission is given for you to make copies of this material for your group only, not for every youth group in your state. Thank you for your cooperation.

Introduce the topic. In most cases, it is important to introduce, or "set up," the topic before you pass out the TalkSheets to your group. Any method will do as long as it is short and to the point. Be careful not to "over-introduce" the subject. Don't use an introduction that is too "preachy" or which resolves the issue before you get started. You want only to stimulate interest and instigate discussion. That is the primary purpose of the introduction.

The simplest way to introduce the topic is verbally. You can tell a story, share an experience, or describe a conflict having to do with the subject. You might ask a simple question, such as, "What is the first thing you think of when you hear the word _____?" (whatever the topic is). After some have volunteered a few answers, you could reply, "It sounds like we all have different ideas on the subject; let's investigate it a bit further," or something similar. Then you distribute the TalkSheets, make certain everyone has a pen or pencil, and you're on your way.

Here are some ways of introducing any of the topics in this book, all of which, of course, should be pertinent:

1. Show a short film or video.
2. Read an interesting passage from a book or magazine article.
3. Play a popular record dealing with the theme.
4. Present a short skit or dramatic reading.
5. Play a simulation game or role play.
6. Present some current statistics, survey results, or read a recent newspaper article.
7. Use an "icebreaker," such as a humorous game. For example, if the topic is "Fun," play a game to begin the discussion. If the topic is "Success," consider a game whose players experience success or failure.
8. Use posters, slides, or any other audio-visual aids available to help concentrate focus.

There are, of course, many other possibilities. The introduction of the topic is left to your discretion and good judgment. You are limited only by your own creativity. Suggestions are offered with each TalkSheet, but they are not mandatory for success. Remember that the introduction is an integral part of each session. It helps set the tone and will influence the kinds of responses you receive. Don't "load" the introduction to the point that the "answer" is revealed, and the students feel hesitant about sharing their own opinions.

Give students time to work on their TalkSheet. After you introduce the topic, pass out a copy of the TalkSheet to each member of the group. Members should also have a Bible, as well as writing implements. There are usually five or six activities on each TalkSheet. If time is limited, direct your students' interest to the specific part of the TalkSheet in which you wish them to participate.

Decide whether or not they should complete the TalkSheet on an individual basis or in groups. Encourage your group to consider what the Bible has to say as they complete their TalkSheets.

Announce a time limit for their written work, then make them aware when one or two minutes remain. They may need more time, or less. Use your own judgment, depending upon your observations of the majority of the group. The discussion is now ready to begin.

Lead the discussion. In order for the TalkSheets to be used effectively, all members of your group need to be encouraged to participate. You can foster a climate that is conducive to discussion by communicating that each person's opinion is worthwhile and each has a responsibility to contribute to the rest of the group. A variety of opinions is necessary for these TalkSheets to have meaning.

If your group is large, you may want to divide it into smaller groups of six to twelve persons each. One person in each smaller group should be appointed facilitator to keep the discussion alive. The facilitator can be either an adult or another young person. Advise the leaders not to try and dominate the group, but to be on the same level with each member. If the group looks to the facilitator for the "answer," have the leader direct the questions or responses back to the group. Once the smaller groups have completed their discussions, have them reassemble into one large group, move through the items again, and ask the different groups to summarize what they learned from each activity.

It is not necessary to divide up into groups every time TalkSheets are used. Variations provide more interest. You may prefer, at times, to have smaller groups of the same sex.

The discussion should center around the questions and answers on the TalkSheet. Go through them one at a time, asking volunteers to share how they responded to each item. Have them compare their answers and brainstorm new ones in addition to those they wrote down. Allow those who don't feel comfortable revealing their answers to remain silent.

Don't feel pressured to spend time on each activity. If time does not permit a discussion of every item, feel free to focus attention only on those provoking the higher interest.

Move with your own creative instinct. If you discover a better or different way to use the activity, do so. Don't feel restricted by the Leader's Instructions on the back of the TalkSheet. Use Scriptures not found on the TalkSheet. Add your own items. TalkSheets were designed for you to be able to add your own thoughts and ideas.

If the group begins digressing into an area that has nothing to do with the topic, guide them back on track. However, if there is a high degree of interest in this side issue, you may wish to allow the extra discussion. It may meet a need of many in the group, and therefore would be worth pursuing.

More information on leading discussions is found in the next section.

 Wrap up the discussion. This is your chance to challenge the group. When considering your closing remarks, ask yourself the following question: What do you want the group to remember from this experience? If you can answer in two or three sentences, then you have your closing remarks. It is important to bring some sort of closure to the session without negating the thoughts and opinions expressed by the group. A good wrap-up should affirm the group and offer a summary that helps tie the discussion together. Your students should be left with the desire to discuss the issue further, among themselves or with a leader. Tell your group members you are available to discuss the issue privately after the meeting. In some cases, a wrap-up may be unnecessary; just leave the issue hanging and bring it up again at a later date. This allows your students to wrestle with the issues on their own. Later, resolutions can evolve.

 Follow up with an additional activity. The Leader's Instructions on the back of the TalkSheet provide you with ideas for additional activities. They are optional but highly recommended. Their purpose is to afford an opportunity to reflect upon, evaluate, review, and integrate what has been learned. Most of your TalkSheet discussions will generate a desire to discuss the subject matter again, which leads to better assimilation and more learning.

Assign the activity and follow up on the assignment with a short, debriefing talk at the next group meeting. Appropriate questions about the activity would be:

1. What happened when you did this activity? Was it helpful or a waste of time?
2. How did you feel while you were doing the activity?
3. Did the activity change your mind or affect you in any way?
4. In one sentence, tell what you learned from this activity.

HOW TO LEAD A TALKSHEET DISCUSSION

The young people of today are growing up in a world of moral confusion. The problem facing youth workers in the church is not so much how to teach the church's doctrines, but how to help kids make the right choices when faced with so many options. The church's response to this problem has traditionally been to indoctrinate—to preach and yell its point of view louder than the rest of the world. This kind of approach does not work in today's world. Teenagers are hearing a variety of voices and messages, most of which are louder than those they hear from the church.

A TalkSheet discussion is effective for just this very reason. While discussing the questions and activities on the TalkSheet, your students will be encouraged to think carefully about issues, to compare their beliefs and values with others, and will learn to make the right choices. TalkSheets will challenge your group to evaluate, defend, explain, and rework their ideas in an atmosphere of acceptance, support, and growth.

CHARACTERISTICS OF A TALKSHEET DISCUSSION

Remember, successful discussions—those that produce learning and growth—rarely happen by accident. They require careful preparation and sensitive leadership. Don't be concerned if you feel you lack experience at this time, or don't have the time to spend for a lengthy preparation. The more TalkSheet discussions you lead, the easier they will become and the more skilled you will be. It will help if you read the material on the next few pages and try to incorporate these ideas into your discussions.

The following suggestions will assist you in reaching a maximum level of success:

 Create a climate of acceptance. Most teenagers are afraid to express their opinions because they are fearful of what others might think. Peer approval is paramount with teenagers. They are fearful of being ridiculed or thought of as being dumb. They need to feel secure before they share their feelings and beliefs. They also need to know they can share what they are thinking, no matter how unpopular or wild their ideas might be. If any of your students are submitted to put-downs, criticism, laughter, or judgmental comments, especially if what they say is opposed to the teachings of the Bible or the church or their leader, an effective discussion will not be forthcoming.

For this reason, each TalkSheet begins with a question or activity less threatening and more fun than some of the questions that follow. The first question helps the individuals to become more comfortable with each other and with the idea of sharing their ideas more openly.

When asking a question, even one that is printed on the TalkSheet, phrase it to evoke *opinions*, not *answers*. In other words, if a question reads, "What should Bill have done in that situation?", change it to, "What *do you think* Bill should have done?" The addition of the three words "do you think" makes the question a matter of opinion rather than a matter of knowing the right answer. When young people realize their opinions are all that are necessary, they will be more apt to feel comfortable and confident.

 Affirm all legitimate expressions of opinion from your group members. Let each person know his or her comments and contributions are appreciated and important. This is especially true for those who rarely participate. When they do, make a point of thanking them. This will encourage them and make them feel appreciated.

Keep in mind affirmation does not necessarily mean approval. Affirm even those comments that seem like heresy to you. By doing so, you let the group know everyone has the right to express their ideas, no matter what they are. If someone does express an opinion that you believe is way off base and needs to be corrected, make a mental note of the comment and present an alternative point of view in your concluding remarks, in a positive way. Do not attack or condemn the person who made the comment.

 Discourage the group from thinking of you as the "authority" on the subject. Sometimes young people will think you have the right answer to every question and they will watch for your reaction, even when they are answering someone else's question. If you find the group's responses are slanted toward your approval, redirect them to the whole group. For example, you could say, "Talk to the group, not to me" or "Tell everyone, not just me."

It is important for you to try to let them see you as a *facilitator*—another member of the group who is helping make the discussion happen. You are not sitting in judgment of their responses, nor do you have the right answer to every problem.

Remember, with adolescents, your opinions will carry more weight the less of an authority figure you appear to be. If you are regarded as an affirming friend, they will pay much more attention to what you have to say.

Actively listen to each person. God gave you one mouth and two ears. Good discussion leaders know how to listen. Your job is not to monopolize the discussion, or to contribute the wisest words on each issue. Keep your mouth shut except when you are encouraging others to talk. You are a facilitator. You can express your opinions during your concluding remarks.

Do not force anyone to talk. Invite people to speak out, but don't attempt to force them to do so. Each member should have the right to pass.

Do not take sides during the discussion. Hopefully, you will have disagreements in your group from time to time with students who will take opposing viewpoints. Don't make the mistake of siding with one group or the other. Encourage both sides to think through their positions and to defend their points of view. You might ask probing questions of both, to encourage deeper introspection of all ideas. If everyone seems to agree on a question, or if they seem fearful of expressing a controversial point, it might be beneficial for you to play "devil's advocate" with some thought-provoking comments. This will force them to think. Do not give them the impression that the other point of view is necessarily your own, however. Remain neutral.

Do not allow one person (including yourself) to monopolize the discussion. Almost every group has that one person who likes to talk and is perfectly willing to express an opinion on every question. Try to encourage everyone to participate.

Arrange seating to encourage discussion. Theater-style seating, that is in rows, is not conducive to conversation. If you must use chairs at all, arrange them in a circular or semi-circular pattern.

Occasionally, smaller groups of four to six persons are less threatening to teenagers, especially if there is a variety of maturity levels in the group. If you have both junior high level and senior high level in the same group, it might be preferable to segregate them accordingly.

Allow for humor when appropriate. Do not take the discussion so seriously as to prohibit humor. Most TalkSheets include questions that will generate laughter as well as some intense dialogue.

Don't be afraid of silence. Many discussion leaders are intimidated by silence in the group. Their first reaction is to fill the silence with a question or a comment. The following suggestions may help you handle silence more effectively:

a. Learn to feel comfortable with silence. Wait it out for thirty seconds. Give someone a reasonable time to volunteer a response. If you feel it appropriate, invite a specific person to talk. Sometimes a gentle nudge is all that is necessary.

b. Discuss the silence with the group. Ask them what the silence really means. Perhaps they are confused or embarrassed and don't feel free to share their thoughts.

c. Answer the silence with questions or comments about it. Occasionally, comments such as "It's a difficult issue to consider, isn't it?" or "It's scary to be the first to talk" may break the ice.

d. Ask a different question that might be easier to handle or that might clarify the one that has been proposed. But don't do this too quickly. Wait a short while first.

Try to keep the discussion under control. Frequently a discussion can become sidetracked onto a subject you may not consider desirable. If someone brings up a side issue that generates a lot of interest, you will need to decide whether or not to pursue that issue and see where it leads, or redirect the conversation back to the original subject. Sometimes it's a good idea to digress—especially if the interest is high and the issue worth discussing. In most cases, however, it is advisable to say something like "Let's come back to that subject a little later, if we have time. Right now, let's finish our discussion on . . . "

Be creative and flexible. Don't feel compelled to ask every question on the TalkSheet, one by one, in order. If you wish, ask only a couple of them, or add a few of your own. The Leader's Instructions may give you some ideas, but think of your own as well. Each question may lead to several others along the same lines, which you can ask during the discussion.

Be an "askable" discussion leader. Make certain your young people understand they can talk to you about anything and find concern and support, even after the TalkSheet discussion has been completed.

Know what your goals are. A TalkSheet discussion should be more than just a "bull session." TalkSheets are designed to move the conversation toward a goal, but you will need to identify that goal in advance. What would you like the young people to learn? What truth would you like them to discover? What is the goal of the session? If you don't know where you're going, it is doubtful you will arrive.

GROUND RULES FOR AN EFFECTIVE TALKSHEET DISCUSSION

A few ground rules will be helpful before beginning your TalkSheet discussions. Rules should be kept to a minimum, but most of the time young people will respond in a positive manner if they know in advance what is expected of them. The following are suggestions for you to consider using:

What is said in this room stays in this room. Confidentiality is vitally important to a healthy discussion. The only time it should be broken is if a group member reveals he or she is going to do harm to himself or herself, to another person, or is being harmed in some way.

No put-downs. Mutual respect is important. If someone disagrees with another's comment, he or she should raise his or her hand and express an opinion of the comment, but not of the person who made it. It is permissible to attack ideas, but not each other.

There is no such thing as a dumb question. Your youth and adult leaders must feel free to ask questions at any time. Asking questions is the best way to learn.

No one is forced to talk. Let everyone know they have the right to remain silent about any question.

Only one person talks at a time. This is one way to teach young people mutual respect. Each person's opinion is worthwhile and deserves to be heard.

If members of the group violate these rules during the discussion or engage in disruptive or negative behavior, it would be wise to stop and deal with the problem before continuing.

THE BIBLE AND TALKSHEETS

Unlike previous TalkSheet books where Scripture was brought in to provide context to the topical discussion, this volume of TalkSheets is centered around key passages in Psalms and Proverbs. Utilizing vital topics as hooks, these TalkSheets are designed to provide you with a creative way to help your kids to dig more deeply into the Bible.

A WORD OF CAUTION . . .

Many of the TalkSheets in this book deal with topics which may be sensitive or controversial. Discussing subjects such as abortion or even materialism may not be appreciated by everyone in the church. Whenever you encourage discussion on such topics, or encourage young people to express their opinions (on any subject) no matter how off base they may be, you risk the possibility of criticism from parents or other concerned adults in your church. They may believe you are teaching the youth group heresy or questionable values.

The best way to avoid problems is to use good judgment. If you have reason to believe a particular TalkSheet is going to cause problems, think twice before you use it. Sometimes the damage done by going ahead outweighs the potential good.

Another way to avoid misunderstanding is to provide parents and others to whom you are accountable with copies of the TalkSheet before you use it. Let them know what you hope to accomplish and the type of discussion you will be encouraging.

It would also be wise to suggest your young people to take their TalkSheet home and discuss it with their parents. They might want to ask their parents how they would answer some of the questions.

WHICH WAY DO I GO ?

 1 Have you ever been lost? Maybe it was at the grocery store when you were little. Perhaps you were in the car with your folks, driving around in circles. Tell the group about it, answering the following questions:

What were you looking for? (Your mom, gym class and so forth.)
How did you lose it?
What was the first thing you tried to help you find it?
If that didn't work, what did?

 2 **Read Psalm 1.** List four things someone like you should do (or not do) to be blessed:

Verse 1: Do not walk _____
Do not stand _____
Do not sit _____

Verse 2: Delight in and think about the _____

 3 Sherri wants to go over to her boyfriend's house against her folks' wishes. Sherri dials her friend Diane and says, "Call my mom and tell her you want me to come over to your house tonight to help you with homework. She won't know it's a trick!"

What principle or principles from Psalm 1 would Diane break if she encourages Sherri to tell her the whole plan?_____

What principle or principles would Diane break if she carries out Sherri's scheme?
_____

What bad things could happen if the two girls carry out the plan?
_____

Is there anything that might seem good that could happen?
_____

What might happen if Diane chooses to not to go along with Sherri's request?
_____

If Diane decides to go God's way, what are some things she could say to Sherri to help her?
_____

 4 In one or two sentences, write an idea for a situation you or someone like you might face; a situation where a choice between good and bad must be made. Here are some ideas: shoplifting, gossiping, lying, fighting, and drugs. You can also list positive situations like befriending a new kid, helping out at a church cleanup day, and so forth.

_____

_____

WHICH WAY DO I GO?

Topic: Choosing to go God's way.
Biblical Basis: Psalm 1

Purpose of this Session:
When it comes down to it, the real reason we work with kids is to help them to choose to live as God would have them. It is appropriate, then, that the first psalm speaks directly to this issue. This TalkSheet gives your students a clear picture of the two roads they can follow in life—God's way or the other—and provides an opportunity for them to choose to go God's way.

To Introduce the Topic:
Show a photograph of (or describe) someone whom your students would recognize as an outstanding success in some field, such as athletics. Do the same for a vile criminal (there are plenty to choose from in the latest headlines). Let your students tell how they think these individuals came to be at the top (or bottom) of their "profession." Point out, "I realize probably none of us in this room will become the world's greatest athlete or the foulest criminal. Still, the choices we make in life do lead us down certain paths. Life is full of crossroads where we must decide what turn to take. Not all decisions are easy ones. Happily, the Bible gives some good advice on how to choose the right path in life."

The Discussion:
Item #1: Break your group into pairs or threes for this segment. Be sure each pair or threesome has at least one person who can remember being lost. When the groups have finished their discussions, have students share their answers to the TalkSheet's question with the entire class. Jot the pertinent principles involved on a chalkboard: "I ran off in the wrong direction," "We missed a landmark," "We stopped to ask directions," etc. Point out how each relates to going the wrong way or finding the right way.
Item #2: Discuss the principles Psalm 1 gives for making wise and godly decisions. Verse 1 speaks against lending an open ear to tempting words, following others into sin, and mocking (ridiculing or ignoring) God. The second verse talks about the wisdom of basing decisions on God's wisdom, found in the Bible. Promises, both positive and negative, are made in verses 3-6. List the Biblical principles for wise decision making on the chalkboard in preparation for the next item.
Item #3: This discussion activity can be done in small groups or with the entire class. Point out that any "good" things that seem to result from disobeying God's principles always have bad results, whether we notice them or not. For example, disobeying God once can be the beginning of a pattern of disobedience. On the other hand, choosing to go God's way whether we want to or not helps to establish godly habits that lead to blessings and rewards in the long run.
Item #4: Try some simple skits based on the situations they describe. Call a few volunteers to act out the parts while you ad-lib a narration. Have the audience suggest right or wrong ways to go in each situation and have your volunteers act them out. The skits can end with possible results of right and wrong choices. After each skit, let everyone discuss how the wisdom of Psalm 1 figures into these situations.

To Close the Session:
Have each student privately think of an area in which he or she needs to jump onto God's road. Distribute index cards (or use the back of the TalkSheet) on which students are to draw a typical road sign (stop sign, yield, green light, one way, wrong way) that can be used to express their thinking. For example, someone might write, "I will YIELD to God's wisdom and STOP skipping classes."
Encourage students to post their cards at home.

Outside Activity:
Create a book titled, "We Went God's Way!" Here's how: Give each student one piece of notebook paper. During the week, each person must do something he or she knows God would want him or her to do (or choose to not do something wrong). That decision—along with any comments the student may wish to make—is written on the page. All the pages are collected and put into a binder to complete the book. A student can remain anonymous if he or she desires, but signed pages are the best. A phone call before the next meeting will help remind students of this assignment.

When Things Go Wrong

1 Life can make you nervous at times! Check out this list of things that can test your deodorant. Rate the items according to how scary you think the average kid like you would find them. Circle "one bucket of sweat" for the least scary, "eight buckets of sweat" for the most scary.

The first time you have to undress in front of other kids in PE class.

Being asked to dance when you know you're an awkward klutz.

Being pressured to swig some beer at a party.

Being told to meet the school bully after class.

Attending a school where kids carry concealed weapons.

Walking through a gang neighborhood wearing the wrong colors.

Forgetting your lines in the school play.

2 Read whichever of the following Bible passages your leader assigns you. Be prepared to tell the rest of the class what happened in that passage.

2 Samuel 15:1-6	**2 Samuel 16:5-14**	**2 Samuel 18:5-17**
2 Samuel 15:13-14, 23-25, 30-31	**2 Samuel 18:24-33**	

3 Now read Psalm 3. This was the psalm that King David wrote after the incident with Absalom! David said that even in the midst of the fear and the attacks, he was able to sleep at night. According to David, how was he able to do this? (Circle all you think apply.)

Tranquilizers	Prayer	He knew God was his shield	Warm milk
God encouraged him	Bedtime stories	The Lord sustained him	

4 If you were KD (King David, the famous advice columnist), what would you tell this person?

Dear KD:
When I left elementary school, I knew everyone and had lots of friends. We always had a good time doing things after school. But now I'm a year or two older and in a bigger school. There are lots of kids I don't know. Many of my old friends are now friends with other kids instead of me. Not only that, but I've got skin problems now, and my body is half kid/half adult and all uncoordinated. Help!

In Need of Repair

Dear In Need:

_____

_____

_____

5 Rewrite in your own words one of the following promises:
Matthew 6:25-26   John 16:33   Colossians 3:15   John 14:27   Philippians 4:6-7

_____

_____

WHEN THINGS GO WRONG

Topic: Trusting God.
Biblical Basis: Psalm 3

Purpose of this Session:

During the junior high years, young people experience rapid changes, stress, and confusion. God can get them through it all, serving as a protector and deliverer just as he did to King David so long ago. Students will learn how they can place their confidence in God and find peace in him.

To Introduce the Topic:

Have everyone stand in the center of the room. Explain that you are going to read some statements. Students are to indicate that they agree with a statement by walking to one wall, or that they disagree by walking to another. No one may remain in the center of the room. As you read the following statements, allow students to "vote" after each one, then count the votes and have everyone return to the room's center. Record the votes on a chalkboard.

　　1. The Bible promises that Christians should never have troubles. **2.** The Bible makes it clear that Christians can't find peace from problems until they go to heaven. **3.** Any Christian struggling with problems is not a very good Christian. **4.** Great Christians never have worries because they can just sit back and watch God solve everything. **5.** Even the greatest believers must learn to trust God in times of trouble.

　　Tell your class that these questions will be tackled in today's session.

The Discussion:

Item #1: Let each student work on the list, then hold a class discussion. Which problems seem to cause the most anxiety? Which are common to most or all students? Ask if there are other examples not listed, common to their group.

　　Say something like this: "Even Christians face troubles like these. In fact, Jesus told us in John 16:33, 'I have told you these things, so that in me you may have peace. In this world you will have trouble. But take heart! I have overcome the world.' Peace doesn't mean a lack of problems; it means assurance that God will stand with us and help us work through them."

Item #2: Explain that the students will be looking at David, the greatest king Israel ever had, and his rotten son Absalom. Absalom tried to overthrow David by attacking with an army. Many men were killed.

　　Assign each passage to a group to read. If you have a small class, assign just one or two passages and be prepared to describe what happens in the rest. Each group then summarizes its passage for the class. Discuss the fears David probably felt and the indications that David was still seeking God in all of his troubles. An example of David's fears is found in 2 Samuel 15:14. An example of his trust is found in 2 Samuel 15:25-26.

Item #3: Discuss the things David says about God in Psalm 3: God is a shield, he takes care of us, he answers prayer, he sustains and delivers, he fights on our behalf, and he blesses his people.

　　Pick the top three or four problems from Item #1 and discuss how the characteristics of God might relate in practical ways to these problems.

Item #4: Have your students consider what advice someone with King David's perspective on God would say to the person who wrote this letter.

Item #5: The focus here is for students to leave class knowing the Bible is filled with verses that promise comfort and peace of mind even to kids like them. Encourage them to be encouraged!

To Close the Session:

Give everyone a few minutes to think of one or more areas in which they are troubled. Let them pray silently for God to dawn his peace in their hearts, to be their shield and deliverer. Offer to lend an ear to their problems privately.

Outside Activity:

Have students create an advice column that you can publish as a newsletter. Students poll schoolmates to see what difficulties they face. The results are then paraphrased into anonymous letters to the editor, along with biblical advice from your students.

What God Thinks Of Liars

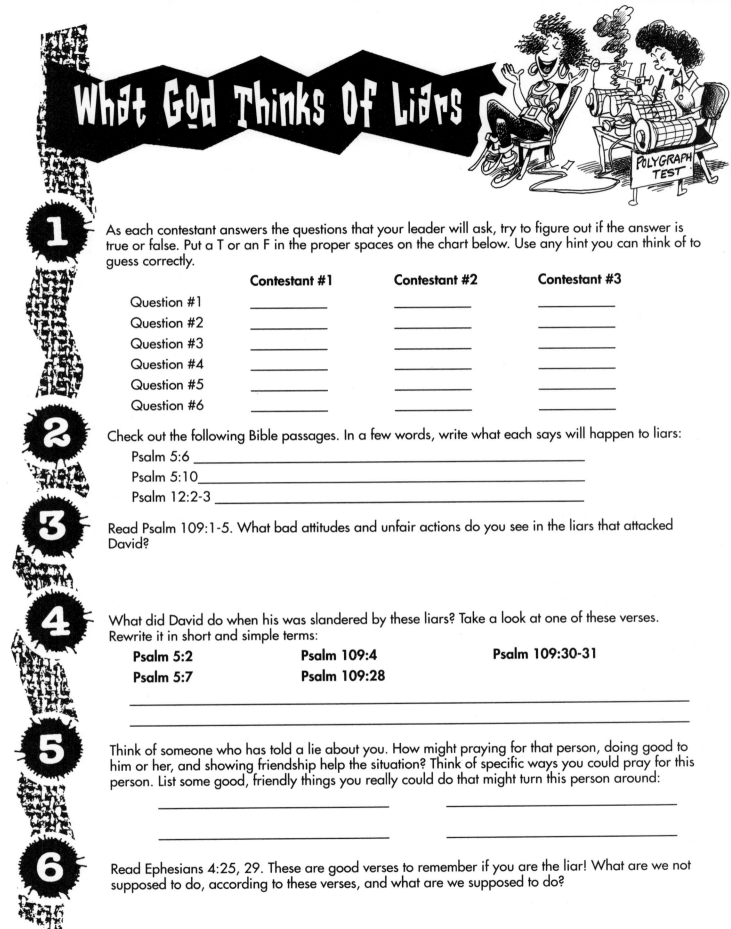

1 As each contestant answers the questions that your leader will ask, try to figure out if the answer is true or false. Put a T or an F in the proper spaces on the chart below. Use any hint you can think of to guess correctly.

	Contestant #1	Contestant #2	Contestant #3
Question #1	_____	_____	_____
Question #2	_____	_____	_____
Question #3	_____	_____	_____
Question #4	_____	_____	_____
Question #5	_____	_____	_____
Question #6	_____	_____	_____

2 Check out the following Bible passages. In a few words, write what each says will happen to liars:

Psalm 5:6 _____

Psalm 5:10_____

Psalm 12:2-3 _____

3 Read Psalm 109:1-5. What bad attitudes and unfair actions do you see in the liars that attacked David?

4 What did David do when his was slandered by these liars? Take a look at one of these verses. Rewrite it in short and simple terms:

Psalm 5:2   **Psalm 109:4**   **Psalm 109:30-31**

Psalm 5:7   **Psalm 109:28**

_____

_____

5 Think of someone who has told a lie about you. How might praying for that person, doing good to him or her, and showing friendship help the situation? Think of specific ways you could pray for this person. List some good, friendly things you really could do that might turn this person around:

_____   _____

_____   _____

6 Read Ephesians 4:25, 29. These are good verses to remember if you are the liar! What are we not supposed to do, according to these verses, and what are we supposed to do?

WHAT GOD THINKS OF LIARS

Topic: Slander.
Biblical Basis: Psalm 5, Psalm 109

Purpose of this Session:

Everyone knows that it is wrong to lie, and it's no fun to be lied about. This TalkSheet will foster an open discussion on lying, being the target of lies, and what God says about it all.

To Introduce the Topic:

Here's a great idea you can try if you have a good sport in class. Tell students something terrible is going on in church. Make up a story about repeated thefts from the church collection plate. It has happened so often that the church staff decided to set a trap to catch the culprit. You and a few other adults watched from hiding places and actually saw someone steal money from the plate. Now you know for sure that someone in this very class is a thief! Say something like, "I'm sorry, John, but I'm going to have to ask you to come with me to the pastor's office." (Name a student that you know is not a thief and can take this shock.)

When John responds and all the students stare, say, "I just told an absolute lie. John is not a thief. There is no stealing going on. What do you think about what I just did?" Explain that you used this shocking attention getter to focus on the subject of lying and being lied about. Apologize to "John."

The Discussion:

Item #1: On an index card write, "Give a lying answer to every question. Try to make your lies sound believable." On another write, "Give a truthful answer to every question." On a third card write, "Lie on the first three questions, tell the truth on the rest. Try to make your lies sound believable." Pick three volunteers to sit at the front of the room. Give each volunteer one of the cards and instruct him or her to do as it says.

Ask the following questions of each volunteer, allowing each to answer the first question before going on to the second, and so on. **1.** Are you related to a famous person? If so, who? **2.** Have you ever won anything worth more than one hundred dollars? If so, what was it? **3.** What is your favorite hobby? **4.** Where is the most interesting place you've ever been? **5.** What is your favorite color? **6.** Have you ever been mentioned in a newspaper or on TV? If so, for what reason?

Reveal which contestant was always telling the truth, which was always lying, and which did both. Students can then check their charts for accuracy. The student who did the best wins.

Explain that some lies are fairly easy to detect, but some are not. Discuss what sort of lies students are likely to hear in the home or at school. Talk about the damage that lies can do to the one who lies as well as the one who is the target of the lies.

Item #2: Have several volunteers share what they've learned from the Scriptures.

Item #3: Discuss and list on a chalkboard.

Item #4: Break your group into pairs and threes. Assign a passage to each pair or threesome. Help students to understand David's response to the liars. He prayed for them, did good to them, and showed them friendship. Though David expressed his desire to see these liars come to ruin, it is important to note that David never tried to bring that about himself. Instead, he turned it over for God to handle.

Item #5: As you discuss this item, caution students to not mention specific names or lies that were told, so that no one is embarrassed.

Item #6: Point out that Ephesians 4:25 speaks about replacing the negative (lying) with the positive (telling the truth). In essence, Paul is telling us how to get rid of a bad habit: Don't just stop it, replace it with something godly. Verse 29 tells us to replace any unwholesome speech (lies, gossip, berating) with words that encourage and build up another person.

To Close the Session:

Sooner or later, every one of your students will be the butt of some lie. Item #4 told them how to handle that. But what should they do if they hear a possible lie about someone else? List these items (and any you think of) on the chalkboard as you discuss them: **1.** Do not pass on the story; **2.** Don't be afraid to challenge the person telling the story; **3.** Talk to the person who is the object of the story. What does he or she say?; **4.** Pray and do good for whoever is at fault.

Outside Activity:

Give your kids a few moments to think of something really good a friend or family member has done that they can tell to others. As an example, perhaps one student knows someone who did volunteer work to help the sick or poor. Encourage the student to pass on that praiseworthy news to others. Let your students also have a moment to think of something they can say that would encourage and build up another person. A kind word and deed can really make a difference.

Valuable To God!

1 Who values you and how do you know? Find out! Simply close your eyes and point to column A below. Whichever phrase your finger lands on, write that in the blank labeled (A). Do this with columns B and C to form a complete—and maybe crazy—answer to the question.

"I know my (A)_____ values me because he or she (B)_____ and (C)_____."

A	B	C
• Mom or Dad	• has raised me my whole life	• works like a slave to provide for me
• best friend	• hangs out at the mall with me	• shares his or her food with me
• little brother or sister	• tries to look just like me	• wants to grow up to be like me
• church youth worker	• prays for me	• laughs at my jokes
• schoolteacher	• lets me take attendance	• once gave me a very nice dunce cap
• dog	• licks my hand	• lets me put a leash on him or her

2 Now read Psalm 8. What is the question David asks in verse 4?

_____

David then lists some wonderful things God has done to show how much he values us (verses 5-8). Circle your favorite:

Made us just one step lower than angels   Crowned us with glory and honor

Made us rulers over the earth   Put us in charge of the earth's resources

3 Read John 3:16. Because of his great love for us, what did God do? What wonderful blessing do we receive? What do your two answers tell you about how valuable you are to God?

_____

_____

_____

4 Check out Romans 8:31-32, then rate, on the scale below, how much you feel God values you:

•————————•————————•————————•————————•————————•
Not at all   **A little bit**   **Pretty much**   **A lot**   **More than I realized**   **Wow!**

5 Circle how you feel knowing that God will always love you:

Stunned   Relieved   Unconcerned
I'll believe it when I see it   Wow!   I have a friend who needs to hear this
This really helps me   Thank you, Lord!   I want to love him more

VALUABLE TO GOD!

Topic: God values us.
Biblical Basis: Psalm 8

Purpose of this Session:

This TalkSheet guides your students to understand that God places high value on each one of them. This value—that comes from God, not our own merits—makes our lives worthwhile and meaningful.

To Introduce the Topic:

Show your students a dollar bill. Ask, "Why is this valuable?" Point out that the dollar is just paper—not much value in and of itself. Describe or show pictures of other things that have no real value other than what we attach to them—a famous painting, an expensive baseball card, and the like. Lead your students to understand that many things are valuable only because people have decided to attach value to them. The world's most expensive painting, for instance, would be of no value at all to a monkey.

Say, "So why are YOU valuable? Let's talk about that. You might find out that you are worth a lot more than you think!"

The Discussion:

Item #1: This tongue-in-cheek approach can be used to turn your students toward serious thoughts about feeling valued by others. Ask them to give some real reasons why they know their families, friends, and others care for them. Then move on to the next item by explaining that God also values them, and very highly. He has gone to great effort to demonstrate that he values each and every person.

Item #2: Allow your students to share their thinking. Try to get them to rephrase David's question in everyday language.

Item #3: By now your students should be convinced that God places a high value on each of them. To ensure this, read Romans 5:8 to your students. Explain that Christ died for us even while we were yet sinners. That is, he loved us even when we were in total rebellion against him.

Item #4: Point out that God's love is based on his nature, not on anything particularly fine about us. It doesn't matter how rich or poor we are, how smart or dumb, or how good-looking or bad-looking. God loves us and is willing to accept us into his kingdom and family if we wish.

Item #5: Let volunteers express their feelings, both positive and negative. Be prepared to follow up with students who express strongly negative or indifferent reactions to this activity.

To Close the Session:

Take a moment to affirm your love for your students. Let them know that they are each of real value to the group, and that you appreciate the thought and feeling they put into the class discussions. Pray for the members of your class, thanking God for demonstrating his love by sending his Son to die for all.

Outside Activity:

Hold a planning session in which students brainstorm practical ways they can demonstrate their high regard for someone special—a friend, family member, or perhaps the pastor of your church.

Why doesn't GOD do something?

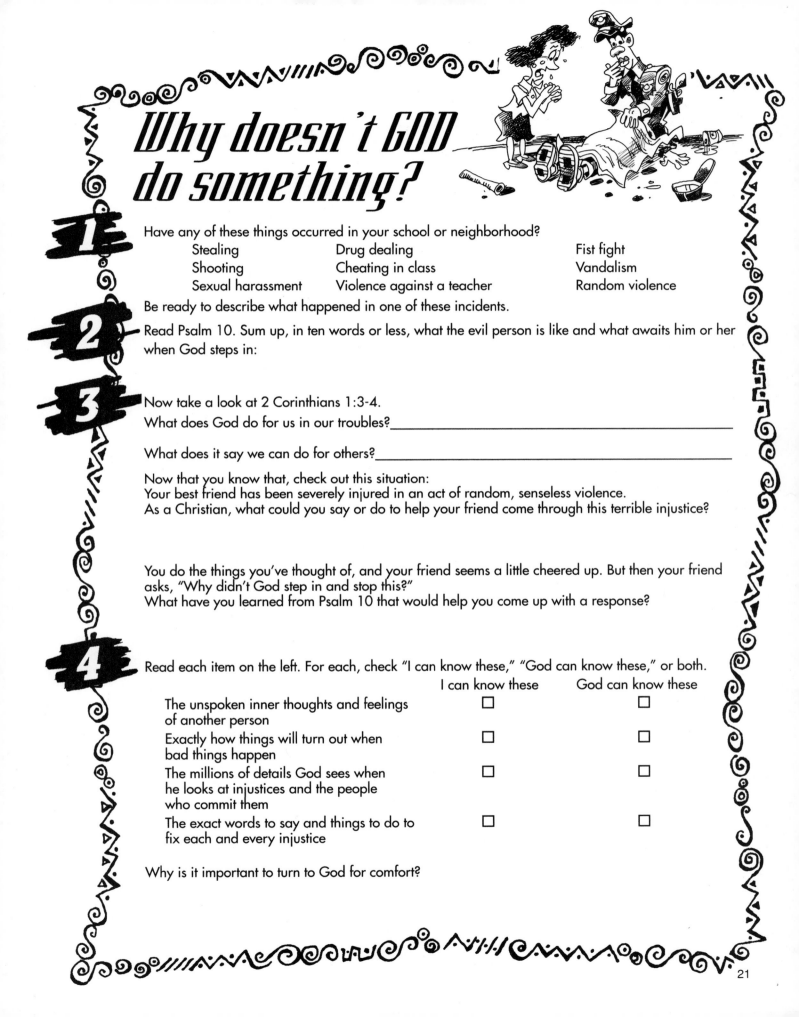

1 Have any of these things occurred in your school or neighborhood?

Stealing	Drug dealing	Fist fight
Shooting	Cheating in class	Vandalism
Sexual harassment	Violence against a teacher	Random violence

Be ready to describe what happened in one of these incidents.

2 Read Psalm 10. Sum up, in ten words or less, what the evil person is like and what awaits him or her when God steps in:

3 Now take a look at 2 Corinthians 1:3-4.

What does God do for us in our troubles?_____

What does it say we can do for others?_____

Now that you know that, check out this situation:
Your best friend has been severely injured in an act of random, senseless violence.
As a Christian, what could you say or do to help your friend come through this terrible injustice?

You do the things you've thought of, and your friend seems a little cheered up. But then your friend asks, "Why didn't God step in and stop this?"
What have you learned from Psalm 10 that would help you come up with a response?

4 Read each item on the left. For each, check "I can know these," "God can know these," or both.

	I can know these	God can know these
The unspoken inner thoughts and feelings of another person	☐	☐
Exactly how things will turn out when bad things happen	☐	☐
The millions of details God sees when he looks at injustices and the people who commit them	☐	☐
The exact words to say and things to do to fix each and every injustice	☐	☐

Why is it important to turn to God for comfort?

WHY DOESN'T GOD DO SOMETHING?

Topic: Life can be unfair.
Biblical Basis: Psalm 10

Purpose of this Session:

By nature, we Christian teachers are optimistic and positive. You can see it in nearly everything we communicate to our students: God loves you, you can have eternal life, he forgives your sins, and so on. But dark days do come, even to believers. This TalkSheet deals with those times when bad people seem to get away with bad things, and God seems slow to respond. Your students will learn that God moves at his own perfect speed and no injustice will go unpunished. They will also discuss ways they can help comfort hurting people.

To Introduce the Topic:

Show or describe current newspaper headlines, featuring bad things that bad people have done. Ask, "Why do you suppose God lets wicked people get away with stuff like this—or does he? What do you think?"

The Discussion:

Item #1: Some of these things have undoubtedly happened in your students' schools and neighborhoods. Let two or three volunteers go into a little detail on what happened, but don't let them go too long or mention names. Ask, "Did any of the people who did these things get away with it or, in your opinion, get off too lightly?" Then say, "The author of Psalm 10 (probably David) wondered why bad people who did bad things sometimes seemed to get off scotfree. Let's take a look."

Item #2: You may wish to read the psalm to your class, or have volunteers read portions. The psalm speaks of the ultimate victory of God over evil and injustice. Ask students to describe how the psalm might offer comfort to the victims of any of the incidents described earlier.

Item #3: Your students can respond to the situation given on the TalkSheet, or use your own questions based on a real situation that students have discussed above. Students should be able to explain that God does keep accounts of wrongs suffered and will eventually set things straight.

Help your learners understand that one of the reasons Christians experience unfair problems may be to prepare us to comfort and help others in similar circumstances.

Item #4: This assignment is designed to assure your students that no one expects them to have all the answers or to know exactly what to say or do when bad things happen to them or their friends. Instead, your students should take comfort in the fact that, because of the promises of Psalm 10, they can confidently tell a victim of injustice that God does care, does take wicked people into account, and will thoroughly punish evildoers. (Many are the times, of course, when God does reveal exactly what to say and do. Encourage your students to look for those times.)

To Close the Session:

Emphasize that sooner or later, each person in the room will suffer unjust hurt or will be called upon to sympathize with and comfort another suffering person. Urge your students to memorize the principles of Psalm 10: Even though wicked people do exist and sometimes prosper, God sees and eventually calls all to account. He also comforts the victim who commits himself or herself to God's loving care.

You may wish to read these promises that amplify Psalm 10's promise of God's retribution: Romans 12:19; Hebrews 10:30-31. And when God seems to be moving in slow motion, try 2 Peter 3:8-9.

Outside Activity:

Videotape one or more segments of the local or network television news that show bad things happening to innocent victims. View the tape with your students and discuss various things Christians could have done or could do now that would help justice be served.

It may be possible for your students to actually lend a hand in righting a wrong they see on the tape. Perhaps they watched a story of someone who was injured due to the disregard or recklessness of another; letters of kindness to the victim or a fund-raiser organized by your group could help to ease the suffering of that person, and perhaps lead them to God.

HOW TO BE A FULL-ON FOOL

1 Rank the following actions from the most foolish (10) to the least foolish (1):

_____ **Sneezing with your mouth full**
_____ **Running into a door at school**
_____ **Smoking cigarettes**
_____ **Throwing an egg at a Hell's Angel**

_____ **Not reading or obeying the Bible**
_____ **Picking your nose and licking your finger**
_____ **Cheating on a test**
_____ **Spilling your cafeteria tray**

2 Read Psalm 14.

What does verse 1 say is inside a fool's heart?

What does verse 2 say about the contents of a fool's head? That is, how does he or she rate in the understanding department?

What does verse 3 say about the direction a fool points his or her feet?

3 Read what the foolish man did in Matthew 7:26-27. Why would that be the same as ignoring Jesus' words?

4 Based on what you've learned today, write out a one-sentence definition of what a fool is, according to God:

5 Now that you know what a fool is, take a look at the following Bible verses to see some of the things a fool does. Draw a line from each passage on the left to its matching idea on the right.

Proverbs 10:8	Shows everyone how stupid he is
Proverbs 10:18	Talks too much and comes to ruin
Proverbs 10:23	Is reckless
Proverbs 12:15	Enjoys evil conduct
Proverbs 12:16	Wastes money
Proverbs 14:1	Never admits he's wrong
Proverbs 14:9	Lives a self-destructive life
Proverbs 14:16	Is hot-tempered
Proverbs 15:5	Spreads slander (gossips)
Proverbs 17:16	Ignores parental discipline
Proverbs 18:2	Doesn't take care of his own life
Proverbs 21:20	Doesn't save or plan for the future
Ecclesiastes 4:5	Likes to blab his own uninformed opinions
Ecclesiastes 10:3	Won't listen to advice

Are any of these problems your problem? Place a check mark next to any that you've tripped over.

HOW TO BE A FULL-ON FOOL

Topic: The fool ignores God.
Biblical Basis: Psalm 14

Purpose of this Session:

No kid wants to be a fool! But the way kids define a fool is different from the way God defines it. To teens, a fool is a nerd, a thief who gets caught, a sucker, an ugly dresser, a klutz, or the like. To God, a fool is someone who ignores him. Despite its title, this TalkSheet will give you and your class insights into how *not* to be a fool in God's eyes.

To Introduce the Topic:

One at a time, hold up the following objects so everyone can see: A large denomination bill, a toothbrush and toothpaste, and a picture or drawing of a stop sign or speed limit sign. Tell students to pretend they are the biggest fools on the planet. Ask them, as fools, how they would treat or respond to the objects you displayed. The idea you are looking for is this: A fool stupidly ignores or mishandles things like money, hygiene, and safety. Tell the group that there is one other thing that fools stupidly ignore—they'll learn what it is during the discussion. They will learn what a fool really is, and how not to be one.

The Discussion:

Item #1: Discuss the students' responses. Point out that although wasting money, having bad breath, driving over the speed limit, and all of the rest are certainly dumb, ignoring God and his Word is by far the most foolish thing a person can do. It not only adversely effects his or her life on earth, but life in eternity too.

Item #2: The passage tells us that a fool's heart is filled with unbelief, his head is filled with lack of understanding, and his feet are taking him away from God. Discuss the meaning of each answer. The third verse might prove particularly controversial since many people today would question God's statement that "there is no one who does good, not even one." After asking students' opinions, remind them that God's definition of a good person is someone equal in goodness and sinlessness to his Son, Jesus Christ.

Item #3: Discuss the imagery that Jesus used: the lack of surefootedness, the pressures, the failure. Make sure students note that it is not just hearing Christ's words but obeying them that makes the difference.

Item #4: Let volunteers read their definitions of a fool.

Item #5: This activity covers a lot of passages, but is well worth the effort. To keep the exercise short, assign each verse to a volunteer reader, then the whole class can decide what the match-ups are.

Discuss the following questions: Are these common problems among teens? Would a person who behaved in these ways be considered a fool by most teens? What is the opposite of each foolish action? Do your students know people who set positive examples by doing the positive things?

To Close the Session:

Point out the progression of foolishness: (1) disbelieve or ignore God; (2) disobey God; (3) wind up doing the things fools do. Explain that the only way not to be a fool in God's eyes is to open up to him, read the Bible, and do what it says.

Encourage students to read their Bibles daily by working with them to come up with a reasonable Bible reading assignment. For example, you might have students commit to reading anything from one verse a day for a month (for poor, unmotivated readers) to a chapter or more each day. Have students write their commitments on a piece a paper for you to collect. Be sure to follow up in the coming weeks.

Outside Activity:

Have each student pick one area from the list of things a fool does that he or she has trouble with (laziness, arguments, gossip, and so forth). Let them choose a time frame (week, two weeks, etc.) within which they will work hard to overcome that problem. If you call each teen to see how they are doing, you will find that you can be an encouragement to them and learn to know them more deeply at the same time.

How To Be A Super Winner!

 Imagine three people: A super athlete, a super model and a super rock star. In the list of talents and traits below, put an A next to all those that would make an athlete a super winner. Do the same for a model (M), and a rock star (RS). Some traits may get more than one initial; some may have none.

_____ Great singing voice	_____ The right clothes
_____ Super good looks	_____ Super intelligence
_____ Big muscles	_____ Good teeth
_____ Good hand-eye coordination	_____ Poetic
_____ Shiny, healthy hair	_____ Good musician
_____ Great "stage presence"	_____ Strong bones
_____ Clear skin	_____ Loud voice
_____ Photogenic	_____ Stamina

 Write a C next to all the above traits that you think would make a Christian a super winner in God's sight.

Read Psalm 15. The psalm lists the traits that God looks for in people. List the traits mentioned in the following verses:

Verse 2: _____ and _____ and _____.

Verse 3: _____ and _____ and _____.

Verse 4: _____ and _____ and _____.

Verse 5: _____ and _____.

 Is it possible for our super model, super athlete, and super rock star to have none of the traits mentioned in Psalm 15 and still be super successful in their line of work? How? Is it possible for a Christian to have none of these traits and be a godly person? How?

 Put a check mark by each godly trait you think you are doing well at. Print your initials by the godly traits you want to work on.

HOW TO BE A SUPER WINNER!

Topic: Godliness.
Biblical Basis: Psalm 15

Purpose of this Session:

Sports heroes, rock stars, Hollywood celebs—are these people winners? God has a different definition. A good example of what he calls a winner is given in Psalm 15. This TalkSheet provides you with an opportunity to set some young lives on the right path to real success.

To Introduce the Topic:

Offer a simple prize (dollar bill, candy bar, or soda) to the student who can most nearly guess your weight. When you have determined the winner, make a great show of praising his or her wonderful winning ways and, tongue-in-cheek, make everyone else aware that they are losers. Restore calm and explain that it's often true that in order for someone to win, someone else must lose. Ask your students to think of situations in which there are losers as well as winners (sports, contests, job opportunities, and the like). Thank everyone for their participation. Then say, "This topic of winning and losing is really interesting to me. I want to be a winner and I want you to be winners. Let's discuss what winning really is, and see if some of the ideas we have of winning might be a bit messed up."

The Discussion:

Item #1: Discuss students' answers, then ask them to name famous "super winners" who have some of the traits listed. It's likely no one will mention a Bible character. If they don't, point this out and ask students if they think there are no winners in the Bible. Then have them work on the next item.

Item #2: Explain that God has a list of traits that he admires in people, but they are considerably different than those listed in Item #1. (None of the traits there match the godly characteristics of Psalm 15.)

Item #3: This exercise will help your young people recognize that the world's definition of a winner is extremely different than the things God values in a person.

   Note: Students will probably wonder about verse 4, which speaks of despising a vile man. We know from the rest of the Bible that it is not hatred we harbor in our hearts for another, but a strong refusal to be in partnership with the sins of others. As you discuss each trait, be sure to define them in modern terms your teens can understand.

Item #4: Allow students time to think this through and respond. Tell them, "It's plain to see that the traits listed at the top of the page are very different from the godly traits. For example, which set of traits would tend to last a whole lifetime and which set tends to disappear with age? Which set is mostly outside appearance and which set comes from the inside of a person? Which set is based on natural talents that people are born with, and which set can anyone enjoy who is willing to do what God wants?"

Item #5: Give volunteers an opportunity to tell which traits they would like to develop.

To Close the Session:

Have each student choose one godly characteristic and design a tattoo on the back of their TalkSheet that expresses their feelings. Artistic ability is not important. Encourage each to put his or her tattoo on a bedroom wall, inside a locker door, or on the cover of a textbook to serve as a reminder of the winning characteristics of a godly person.

   Here's another idea: Have students each write their choice of a godly trait on a slip of paper. Collect the papers, put them in a hat or other container, and let students draw them out. Each student is to prayerfully consider how well he or she demonstrates that characteristic. Encourage everyone to work on their characteristics during the coming week.

Outside Activity:

Assign students the task of finding articles about famous people in those weekly "gossip tabloids" available at grocery checkout counters. The articles should feature a photograph of the person and dwell on how miserable the person is or what horrible things he or she has been up to. These articles are rarely true, but the pictures and stories make a great montage. Have your students bring these articles to your next meeting, at which time you can remind them of the godly traits that are such a contrast to what the tabloids feature.

count your blessings

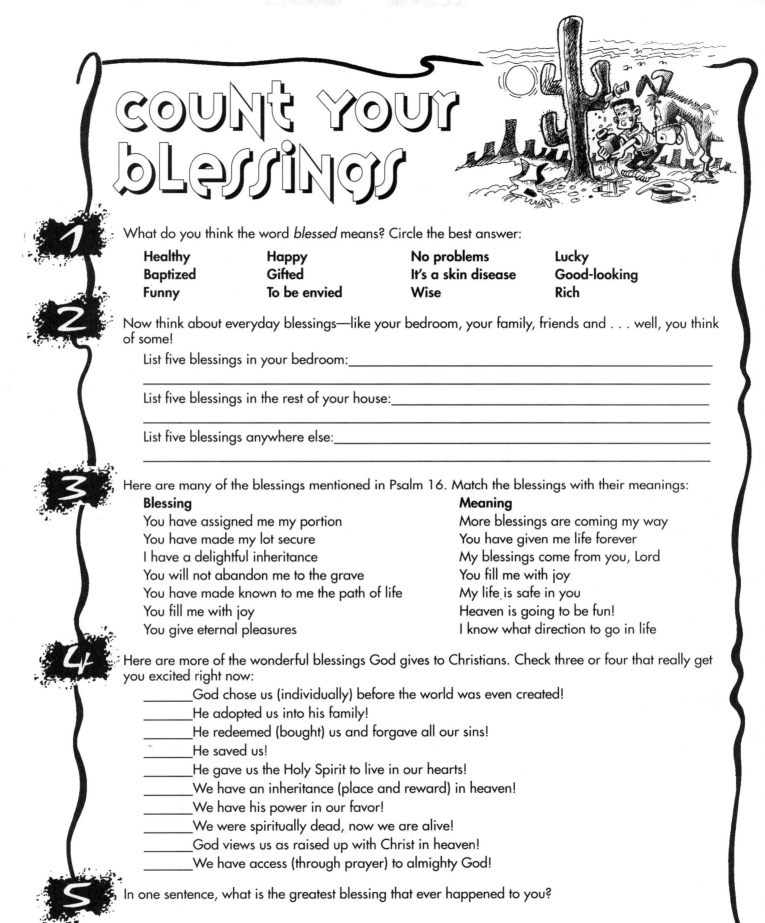

1 What do you think the word *blessed* means? Circle the best answer:

Healthy	Happy	No problems	Lucky
Baptized	Gifted	It's a skin disease	Good-looking
Funny	To be envied	Wise	Rich

2 Now think about everyday blessings—like your bedroom, your family, friends and . . . well, you think of some!

List five blessings in your bedroom:_____

_____

List five blessings in the rest of your house:_____

_____

List five blessings anywhere else:_____

_____

3 Here are many of the blessings mentioned in Psalm 16. Match the blessings with their meanings:

Blessing	Meaning
You have assigned me my portion	More blessings are coming my way
You have made my lot secure	You have given me life forever
I have a delightful inheritance	My blessings come from you, Lord
You will not abandon me to the grave	You fill me with joy
You have made known to me the path of life	My life is safe in you
You fill me with joy	Heaven is going to be fun!
You give eternal pleasures	I know what direction to go in life

4 Here are more of the wonderful blessings God gives to Christians. Check three or four that really get you excited right now:

_____God chose us (individually) before the world was even created!

_____He adopted us into his family!

_____He redeemed (bought) us and forgave all our sins!

_____He saved us!

_____He gave us the Holy Spirit to live in our hearts!

_____We have an inheritance (place and reward) in heaven!

_____We have his power in our favor!

_____We were spiritually dead, now we are alive!

_____God views us as raised up with Christ in heaven!

_____We have access (through prayer) to almighty God!

5 In one sentence, what is the greatest blessing that ever happened to you?

COUNT YOUR BLESSINGS

Topic: Blessings.
Biblical Basis: Psalm 16

Purpose of this Session:

This session provides the opportunity to discuss some of the blessings of knowing Christ and gives you a chance to tell your students why you can say, "My heart is glad and my tongue rejoices" (Psalm 16:9).

We realize that there are times in every life when it is difficult or impossible to feel blessed and happy. Those times are not in view in this TalkSheet. They can be discussed in other sessions.

To Introduce the Topic:

Because the subject today is bright and upbeat, this TalkSheet features some upbeat and tongue-in-cheek activities that should get your students smiling.

To start off, describe or show a jar of dill pickles and a banana. Say something like, "I think of dill pickles as unhappy fruit—or vegetables or whatever they are. They are all wrinkled and warty and sour and green. Bananas, on the other hand, are happy and sunny. See, if I hold this banana sideways, it even looks like it's smiling!" Explain that, while it may be possible for a Christian to look and act like a dill pickle, God really intends for Christians to feel joy over the many blessings he gives us. Tell your students, "I want you to be bananas. Oops! Most of you already are! I mean that I want you to enjoy your Christianity. God has done some wonderful things for us to make us glad. Let's take a look."

The Discussion:

Item #1: Although several of the answers are examples of blessings, the Bible defines the term mainly as happy and to be envied. Christians are in an enviable position because of their relationship with God.

Item #2: You can prime your students' thinking with a few suggestions (clothes, pets, food, money, parents). As the discussion progresses, remind everyone of two things: God is the source of all good blessings, and we should have a thankful attitude for the things he gives us.

Item #3: Discuss each blessing and help students relate them to their lives. Tell students that Psalm 16 is just a tiny sample of the many Bible passages that speak of the wonderful gifts Christians can enjoy. Some class members may be able to think of other blessings mentioned in the Bible.

Item #4: These blessings are found in Ephesians. Have students explain why they chose the ones they did. Be sure everyone understands what each statement means.

Item #5: Let students share their answers. Jot them on the board, then lead your students in prayer, thanking God for each one.

To Close the Session:

Encourage everyone in the group to form a habit of "counting their blessings" and thanking God daily for the goodness he shows them.

Outside Activity:

Collect a stack of magazines from which your students can clip photos, headlines, and drawings that illustrate ordinary and extraordinary blessings that God provides. Make a giant collage.

Victory!

1 Check one or two of your personal goals:

_____ Sports achievement
_____ Good education
_____ Staying drug and alcohol-free
_____ Staying away from sex until marriage
_____ Living a life pleasing to God
_____ Getting through this problem:_____
_____ Entering this career: _____
_____ Other: _____

2 Read Psalm 20. Match the phrases on the left with the correct endings on the right:

May the Lord answer you when	sacrifices
May his name	support
May he send you	burnt offerings
May he grant you	the desire of your heart
May he remember all your	you are in distress
May he accept your	protect you
May he give you	help
May he make all your	requests
May he grant all your	plans succeed

3 Pick one of situations below and answer these questions:

What are two or three things this person must do to achieve the goal?

What are two or three things this person must *not* do to achieve the goal?

How can God help?

• Melissa wants to finish school with high honors. She knows she has to work hard.
• Steve wants to be a track star. But he's not sure he has the discipline.
• Linda wants to stay away from alcohol, but her mom's an alcoholic.

4 Look at Psalm 20:7-8. Decide what message God is sending to you:

5 Write a postcard to God, telling him what your goal or challenge is and how you hope he will help you.

Dear God:

God
Streets of Gold
Cloud 9, Heaven

VICTORY!

Topic: Facing challenge.
Biblical Basis: Psalm 20

Purpose of this Session:

Young people face significant challenges in their daily lives. Some challenges are in the area of temptations: resisting drugs, staying sexually pure, dealing with anger or depression. Other challenges are more positive: striving to do well in school, succeeding in athletics, reaching personal goals. In Psalm 20, David prayed for victory in battle. His prayer shows teens that the best way to face any challenge is at the side of God. This TalkSheet gives your group a chance to see how God's power can help anyone meet life's challenges.

To Introduce the Topic:

Tell your class about a difficult challenge you faced. Tell how God helped you through it or, if you weren't a Christian at the time, how you think God could have played a greater part in your struggle.

Another way to approach the topic of challenge is to present one. Let volunteers arm wrestle, engage in a staring duel, or the like. Tell you class that whenever a person is faced with a challenge, the result is either victory or defeat. God can help us win.

The Discussion:

Item #1: Because some of these goals are highly personal, let the kids know that they need not share their thoughts with the class. But you can discuss whatever ones you like in general ways. Some students will be willing to talk about personal goals. Ask questions like, "What are some of the steps required to meet this goal?" "What are the hardest steps?" "What might you have to give up to meet this challenge?"

Item #2: Discuss every phrase, allowing students to suggest ways each thought relates to the subject. Explain that sacrifices and burnt offerings were ways Old Testament believers honored God. Honoring God is a real key to seeing his presence as one works toward a goal.

Item #3: Assign or allow small groups to pick one of the situations. Help students understand that a goal can be a real challenge—lofty goals are not easily obtained. But God can help in real ways. God could help Melissa achieve her educational goals by giving her the energy she needs to study late, giving her a clear mind and a good memory, and by helping her answer test questions with just the right words. The Lord could provide Steve with a committed coach who could help Steve to stick to his practice program. God could cause Linda to realize that she needs to find non-drinking friends who support her.

Item #4: Have students share their messages.

Item #5: Ask a few volunteers read their postcards.

To Close the Session:

Hang a big piece of paper on the wall and provide several different colored marker pens, or use a chalkboard and chalk. On the top in big letters print, VICTORY! Under that, print the phrase, "God help us to . . . " Give each student a chance to jot a short end to that sentence. You might set the pace by writing, " . . . love You!" Urge everyone to write a real goal that God can help them reach.

Outside Activity:

If someone in your group has an exceptional goal, such as medaling in a school sport or overcoming a severe injury or disease, organize your class into a support group. Let your students determine when and for what they will pray, how they can offer encouragement in tangible ways, what events to attend, and so forth. Be sure your class members realize that God can and will work through their actions.

As an alternative, invite a person who faced a great challenge to describe the experience to your class.

Follow the Leader

1 Try to remember a time when you were a kid when you got lost or separated from your parent. Circle the words that describe how you felt:

Unconcerned	Panicked	Curious	Fearful	Abandoned
Dumb	Shocked	Worried	Confident	Relaxed
Undaunted	Dismayed	Confused	Sad	Alarmed

2 Name a couple of places in the world where you would want a guide with you if you went exploring: _____

_____

3 Do you think people need a guide to get them through life? Yes _____ No _____
Why or why not?

4 Read Psalm 23. Match what God does with the benefit to us:

He is the shepherd	in paths of righteousness
He makes me	comfort me
He leads me	I shall not be in want
He guides me	lie down in green pastures
He is with me	a table before me
His rod and staff	beside quiet waters
He prepares	my cup overflows
He anoints my head	I will fear no evil

5 Go through Psalm 23 again and describe the condition this person would be in if God was NOT his or her shepherd and guide:

_____

_____

6 Who guides you through life? Circle the true answer.

God	My parents	A little of everyone
Myself	My friends	I have no guide

FOLLOW THE LEADER

Topic: Following Christ.
Biblical Basis: Psalm 23

Purpose of this Session:

Life is a journey that none of us have taken before. Those of us who have been on the path long enough real-ize that it is full of pitfalls and dark passages. For many kids, whose travels are just beginning, life is merely a carefree adventure. But a journey as serious and potentially disastrous as the trip through life needs a guide—someone who knows every turn, every safe resting place, every refreshing brook. Kids are miles ahead in life if they start out with the guide who can direct them safely to their destination. That guide is Jesus Christ. Psalm 23 paints a picture of the care and guidance that each of us needs. Submitting to the leading of God is an act of wisdom and personal safety.

To Introduce the Topic:

Have a few willing students try their hands at being "guide dogs." As other willing students are blindfolded, one at a time, your "guide dog" volunteers must get them safely around the room, using only verbal instruc-tions. Use this activity to help your kids to start thinking about the need for guidance as we go through life.

The Discussion:

Item #1: Have a few student volunteers describe their experiences, sharing how they felt and any lessons that they learned. Then describe a time when you were lost as a kid.

Item #2: Point out some places on this earth where most of us would really want to have an experienced guide traveling with us—the Sahara desert, Mount Everest, the Amazon jungle.

Item #3: Discuss the need for a guide through this life. Have your kids brainstorm the qualities that would make the ideal guide, and list those qualities on a chalkboard.

Item #4: After your students have matched the two columns, discuss how these blessings could be redefined in today's terms. Have your kids offer suggestions and list them on the chalkboard.

Item #5: Explore what the state of a person might be like if he or she walks through the same ground as the psalm writer, without the benefit of God's guidance. Discuss how this is similar to people who try to live life without Christ as their Lord.

Item #6: Ask your students to honestly consider who it is that guides them through life. Talk about the wisdom of making God the only voice we listen to for advice on the path of life.

To Close the Session:

Reemphasize the idea that each of us is really a stranger to life. Encourage your students to make Christ their Guide now, while they are young, so that they can avoid getting bogged down in the tar pits, dead ends, and bunny trails that so abound in this life. Explain how God guides us with his word and comforts us with the Holy Spirit.

Outside Activity:

Have your students memorize this popular psalm at home. Let them know that it will be valuable to them all through their lives. Practice reciting this psalm from memory with your kids at future meetings.

When Mom and Dad Let You Down

1 List the three best times you ever had with your folks:

_____
_____
_____

List the three worst times:

_____
_____
_____

2 Answer each of the following questions by filling in the box on the Rate-O-Meter:

	Yes	Sort of	Maybe	Not usually	No
Do your parents trust you?					
Do they listen to you?					
Are they divorced or about to be?					
Does one or both drink too much?					

3 If you have bad parents, there's nothing you can do about it.
Do you agree with this statement?

AGREE   **DISAGREE**

Why or why not?

4 Read Psalm 27:10. This short verse tells us some important things about God! Try these questions on for size:

How do you think God feels about you?_____

What do you think he will do because of his feelings? _____

What won't he do? _____

Is he likely to change his feelings?_____ Why or why not?_____

5 Check out these Bible passages:
Deuteronomy 5:16. I do this by _____

Ephesians 6:1. I do this by _____

Proverbs 1:8-9. I do this! The last thing they taught me is_____

WHEN MOM AND DAD LET YOU DOWN

Topic: Parents.
Biblical Basis: Psalm 27

Purpose of this Session:
For the first time in America, single-parent families outnumber two-parent families. Even teens with two parents often must deal with a stepparent or a mom or dad who is alcoholic, abusive, or distant. This TalkSheet points out that God loves each and every teen. He can fill the void and soothe the pain. In the church, God has provided adult men and women who may fill the role of parent for a needy teen.

To Introduce the Topic:
Work together as a group to dream up an imaginary want ad for the perfect parents. Your teens may suggest things like "very rich," but steer the conversation toward character traits such as loyal, affirming, and so forth. If someone mentions that he or she has great parents, have that student share some of the things that make them successful parents.

The want ad can be jotted on the chalkboard or a large piece of paper. Review it and remark, "Perfect parents are hard to find. Almost everyone has trouble with mom or dad sooner or later. These problems can range from simple disagreements to alcoholism, abuse, and divorce. Let's talk about what God can do to help us with the problems we experience with our parents."

The Discussion:
Item #1: Ask for volunteers to share what they've written. Some students may mention things like, "A really bad time was when Dad lost his job," or "When Mom died of cancer." Although these troubles are not self-inflicted like alcoholism or desertion, they are still real disappointments and are valid for this discussion. Ask kids to describe the feelings and emotions they experienced during their favorite times with their parents. Do the same with the bad times.

Item #2: The Rate-O-Meter results are a good launching pad into deeper discussion. Ask, "How do you feel about your parents right now? Have your relationships with your parents improved, gotten worse, or stayed level over the last few years? What would be the hardest things to do well as a parent? What are some of the frustrations your parents feel?" (Note: Some families may need professional help. If so, most states require you to speak up. Be sure to inform your pastor of any reportable situations.)

Item #3: Discuss what practical steps parents and their children might need to take to solve some of the problems raised above. For example, what might lead to a better relationship in a family where children feel they are not listened to? Scheduled talk times—with the TV and other distractions put aside—is one answer. A regular "date night" or game night allows parents and children to talk comfortably. Doing homework together now and then gives everyone a chance to get in the habit of communicating.

Item #4: Help your students to understand that God loves them. If there are troubled families represented in your group, indicate that God can help. Sometimes he actually changes parents (and children); sometimes he provides comfort even though parents don't change. He can even bring loving Christian adults (such as you) into a teen's life to help heal the pain. Offer to talk privately with anyone who wishes.

Item #5: Have your class read and discuss these passages one at a time. What are some realistic ways these passages can be practiced in the family?

To Close the Session:
Review the main points of the lesson: Parents and children can have struggles; God can offer solutions; children are commanded to honor, obey, and listen to their parents. Tell your students that these issues require prayer. Have everyone write one or two prayer requests for themselves and their parents on slips of paper. These requests should focus on specific problems. They can be anonymous or not. Collect all the slips and pray for them one at a time, or redistribute them for individuals to pray.

Remind students that you are available for private talk. You may wish to take the initiative in some students' lives by inviting them for a one-on-one soda.

Outside Activity:
Organize a Parent Appreciation Event that will get some of those unchurched parents into your fellowship. With a little follow up afterwards, it is very possible that one or more families will become regular attenders. Even those who don't will be touched at the warmth they feel from their children and your ministry.

I LOVE YOU LORD

1 Circle the word or words below that best describe your idea of God:

My Lord and Savior	Old fuddy-duddy	Beard, long gray hair
Big, really BIG!	Far away	I never think much about God
Loving	Creator	Impossible to understand
A big judge	Exciting	Interesting
He lives in my heart	Gladly hears my prayers	I want to know him more and more
Mythology	I want to ask him lots of questions	Really great!

2 Read Psalm 37:4.

What does it say to do?_____

What does it say will happen?_____

3 Write a sentence explaining what you think it means to delight in the Lord:

4 Rate how you feel about these areas:

	YES	NO
I'm glad to be a Christian	☐	☐
I enjoy talking to God	☐	☐
I enjoy talking about God	☐	☐
I like these Bible studies because I can understand them	☐	☐
I can see God working in my life	☐	☐
The idea of heaven is exciting to me	☐	☐
I'd like to serve God with my life	☐	☐
I'm excited about learning more about God and growing as a Christian	☐	☐

5 Now rewrite Psalm 37:4, replacing the word delight with at least five phrases describing ways to delight in God. (See #4 for some ideas.)

I LOVE YOU LORD

Topic: Delighting in God.
Biblical Basis: Psalm 37:4

Purpose of this Session:

"If you love me, you will obey what I command," Jesus says in John 14:15. We teach our students to love God by faithful acts of obedience and service. But what about the emotional aspect of love for God? Psalm 37:4 is perhaps the best short description of a heartfelt love for God: "Delight yourself in the Lord . . . .". This TalkSheet gives your students the opportunity to discover the joys of being delighted by God.

To Introduce the Topic:

Ask your class members to describe in one or two words their emotional responses to things kids really like: jelly donuts, perfect ski or surf conditions, a pet with a cute personality, the first time they received a bike or other great gift, and so on. (You might bring in a box of donuts and juice to get the discussion rolling.) Explain that the Bible often uses a word to describe these sort of emotional feelings: delight. Move into the first TalkSheet activity by explaining that today's topic is delighting in, or enjoying, God.

The Discussion:

Item #1: This helps students come to grips with their view of God. Is he exciting to them? Do they ignore him? This is a good time for you to relate your changing attitude toward God as you came to commit your life to him. Tell your class what God means to you and why.

Item #2: Ask students to share their answers. Be sure they understand that the promise of receiving the desires of their hearts does not mean we can have anything we want anytime we want. The verse means that not only will God give us the object of our desires; he will place his godly desires in our hearts first. Those desires will not be in conflict with his will or nature.

Item #3: Get a good consensus of opinion on this one. Sum it up in a short statement and write it on a chalkboard.

Item #4: This activity provides your students the opportunity to evaluate their "delight factor." Encourage them to get excited about God—learning about him, thinking about him, talking to him, and so forth. Put in a word about the various opportunities your church provides for kids to do these things together.

Item #5: Ask students to share what they have written. Congratulate them for their efforts and jot some of the best on the chalkboard.

To Close the Session:

Give everyone a chance to record a "message to God" on a cassette recorder. Each student gets to say or shout one sentence: "I love you God, because . . . "

Outside Activity:

Plan a "Jesus Celebration Party." Include music that celebrates wonderful things God has done for us (music videos can be nice), several short (one-minute) Bible talks that point out the greatness of God, a time to listen to the audio tape you made, praise posters, Bible games, party favors, cake and ice cream, and so on.

RICH MAN, POOR MAN

1 Here is a list of things that you will leave behind when your life on earth is over. Which ones will you miss the most? Rate them in order, #1 being the one you'd most hate to leave behind:

___The ole neighborhood   ___CD collection   ___The television
___House and bedroom   ___Church   ___Vacations
___A pet   ___Food   ___Car (if you could have one)
___Money   ___Sports   ___Music instrument

2 Read at least one of the following Bible passages. In one sentence, tell the main thought of your passage:

Psalm 49:1-9_____

Psalm 49:10-12_____

Psalm 49:13-15_____

Psalm 49:16-20_____

3 In Luke 12:22-34, Jesus speaks about the things on the left below. The things on the right are what he said about them. Draw lines to match the two lists. Some items in either list may have lines going to more than one item.

Verse	What Jesus speaks about	What Jesus says about them
22-23	Food	God clothes them in splendor
22-23	Clothes	Life is more than these
24	Birds	Are more valuable to God
24	You	Don't worry about it
27	Flowers	Knows that you need material things
29	Your heart	God feeds them 30
30	Pagans (non-Christians)	You must seek this
30	Your Father	They don't work or spin cloth
31-32	His kingdom	Don't set it on food or drink
31	Things you need	God will give you these things
33	Treasure in heaven	They run after material things
		God is pleased to give it to you
		It will never be taken from you

4 What are some practical things you can do to earn reward in heaven? Here are some ideas; circle one or two that you would be willing to try:

Bring a new kid to a fun youth group event   Do a major cleanup of our classroom
Send a Christian get-well card   Join a youth group planning committee
Raise funds for our group at a car wash   Tell a friend about Jesus
Pass out food to the poor   Pray regularly for my youth leaders

Now we want to hear YOUR idea! What is one thing that you could and would do to earn reward in heaven?

RICH MAN, POOR MAN

Topic: Eternal wealth.
Biblical Basis: Psalm 49

Purpose of this Session:

As the bumper sticker says, no hearse tows a U-Haul. If we are doomed to leave all our earthly treasures behind when we go, it makes sense to start investing in the eternal world now. This TalkSheet will provide your students with practical ways to do that.

To Introduce the Topic:

Ask your kids to help you calculate how long it would take to drain the Pacific Ocean with an eyedropper. The Pacific has a surface area of about 64,000,000 square miles and an average depth of about two miles. Multiply those figures to get the volume (128,000,000 cubic miles). One cubic mile equals about 150,000,000,000 cubic feet. 150,000,000,000 times 128,000,000 equals 19,200,000,000,000,000 cubic feet in the ocean. Multiply that times 1,728 cubic inches per cubic foot, and you have 33,000,000,000,000,000,000 cubic inches in the Pacific Ocean! If it takes five eyedroppers to hold a cubic inch, ask your students how many years it would take to empty the ocean at one eyedropper per second. (Round off to 30 million seconds in a year.)

Your students probably will run out of patience long before they solve the problem! Point out that emptying the ocean with an eyedropper, no matter how long it takes, is nothing compared to eternity. Each human being will live in eternity forever. It's best to plan ahead. The Bible tells how.

The Discussion:

Item #1: Ask students to explain their top two or three choices. Point out that people weren't on the list because they will also spend eternity in heaven if they are Christians.

Item #2: Break your group into pairs or threes. Assign each pair or threesome one of the passages. The main thought you want students to uncover in verses 1-9 is that earthly wealth can't buy eternal life. Verses 10-12 speak of the temporary nature of wealth and life on earth. Verses 13-15 note that all die; there is hope only in God's redemption. The final portion states that no matter how wealthy one is, nothing can be taken into eternity.

The upshot of this psalm is that material possessions are no substitute for the eternal life that God offers. To put it in terms that junior highers can understand, having things on earth is nice, but having life in heaven is everything.

Item #3: Before students work on this item, read the parable of the rich fool (Luke 12:16-21). Students can then complete the assignment in groups or as a class discussion. Sum up the main theme of Jesus' message.

Item #4: Have volunteers share some of their ideas, then brainstorm a practical class project that would involve everyone in some sort of heavenly reward-earning work. You can make it as simple or as involved as your students are willing to do. For example, your students might decide to visit a sick senior church member. They can merely knock on the door and express their regards and prayers, or they can go all the way: various teams could cook a meal, straighten up the house, mow the lawn, read a story to the older person, restock the cupboards, wash the towels, and so forth.

To Close the Session:

Have a few volunteers draw a large "Treasure in Heaven" dollar bill on the chalkboard—use your imagination (an angel or two, a treasure chest, a castle in the clouds, or the like). Have students suggest at least ten things that earn reward in eternity, which they jot on the bill. Encourage kids to do these things habitually.

Outside Activity:

If you have decided to do a class project, use the checklist below to organize your students into an effective team. Have students make personal copies of the checklist to remind them of their commitment and duties. Make a master copy. Get everyone's phone number so you can check up on them as the date nears.

CLASS PROJECT: WHO I AM TO DO IT WITH:
WHAT I AM TO DO: THINGS I NEED TO BRING:
WHEN I AM TO DO IT:

GOD WHO?

1 Draw a line to the word in the right column that matches the description in the left column:

Is not sure if there is a God or not **Atheist**
Believes in God, but not sure which one **Agnostic**
Believes that God does not exist **Deist**

2 Circle the things below that you think give evidence for God's existence:

Music	Nature	Babies	The Universe	Our Consciences
Love	Evil	Skyscrapers	Telescopes	Math Logic
Science	History	Disasters	Feelings	Common Sense

3 Do you agree or disagree with the following statements?

Sometimes I doubt that God really exists. **Agree** ___ **Disagree** ___
It would be better if God made himself more obvious. **Agree** ___ **Disagree** ___
God is obvious but people aren't looking or don't care. **Agree** ___ **Disagree** ___

4 Read Psalm 53:1-4, 6. Describe in your own words the problems that people who say there is no God have:

Who is the one who answers the prayer of verse 6?

5 There are good ways and harmful ways we help someone who is doubtful or even foolish in his or her belief about God to reconsider, and put his or her trust in his existence. Cross out the harmful ways to "help" someone believe in God:

Show kindness	Be patient	Argue
Give intelligent answers	Call them stupid	Be an example
Pray for them	Be a hypocrite	Quote Bible verses
Love them	Reason with them	Put them down
Be righteous	Be self-righteous	Be honest
Exclude them	Tell them they are going to hell	Laugh at them

GOD WHO?

Topic: God's existence.
Biblical Basis: Psalm 53

Purpose of this Session:

The idea of God's existence has been debated for centuries. Doubters and skeptics are found even among young teens. On top of those who profess not to believe in God or say they are unsure, there are those who are really practicing atheists. They may verbally acknowledge God's existence, but they act as if he is not alive. This Talksheet is designed to spark thinking and discussion about the existence of God and our way of dealing with those who deny him.

To Introduce the Topic:

Stand by the light switch for this introductory discussion. Ask you students if they have ever seen electricity. (None of them have.) Hit the light switch and ask if they are seeing electricity. Point out that they have never seen electricity but only the results of electricity. Ask how many believe in electricity? Ask how many have felt electricity? Use this as a starting point to show its similarity to our faith in God.

Another approach is to use the idea of gravity, again something we have never seen. Pick a good-natured student to help you illustrate this idea. Have the kid lay on the floor with his or her arms under his or her rear end. Hold an egg over his or her head, and then tell your students that you have come to the conclusion that because you have never seen gravity, there is no such thing. You are now going to "prove" that gravity does not exist. Allow your victim to try to talk you out of dropping the egg by arguing that gravity does exist even if you can't see it. It's up to you whether or not you are convinced enough to not drop the egg.

The Discussion:

Item #1: Discuss what the various phrases and words mean. Make sure that kids know the difference between an atheist (one who believes God does not exist) and an agnostic (one who is not sure).

Item #2: Have your kids share what things most strongly support God's existence for them. Allow kids to explain their positions and add additional items.

Item #3: Ask kids to talk about how they sometimes feel about God's existence or his apparent silence. Talk about the ways God is apparent if we care to look—in the lives of others, through his presence in prayer, through his Word, and the like. Allow kids with real doubts and questions to have them.

Item #4: Discuss the description of the human heart. How is human vileness and corruption in evidence today? Have your kids discuss examples. Point out the hope that has come to us through Christ's birth, death, and resurrection.

Item #5: Discuss the good and harmful ways to convince others that God does indeed exist. Have kids suggest other harmful "assistance" ideas that need to be avoided. Point out that a godly life is the best argument for the existence of the Creator.

To Close the Session:

Summarize the points made about the foolishness of the human heart when it denies God. Point out that those who act as if God does not exist are just a guilty as those who profess he doesn't exist. Discuss the fact that there are solid reasons to believe in God, and that faith is not the same as wishful thinking. Let kids know that it is common to have doubts, but that those doubts can be resolved by taking time to consider the wonders of God, our experience with him, and the inner voice that tells us he really does exist.

Outside Activity:

Invite a person in your church or area who is skilled in presenting evidence on the existence of God to speak to your kids. Make sure this person keeps his or her material simple enough for young teens to understand. Have your kids submit questions in advance that this resource person can try to answer.

WHAT A PAL!

1 Here are things that could happen between friends. Check three that would bother you the most:
Your friend . . .

☐ tells everyone your most embarrassing secret.
☐ steals your girlfriend or boyfriend.
☐ does something wrong and blames you.
☐ asks you to help cheat at school.
☐ dumps you for a new set of friends.
☐ lies to you.
☐ won't admit that he or she borrowed something of yours.
☐ gets you in trouble with your mom.

2 Proverbs 18:24 talks about "a friend who sticks closer than a brother." What do you think makes a good friend? Name three qualities that apply:

_____

_____

_____

3 Read Psalm 55:12-14, 20-21, written by King David. Based on what you read, finish this thought:

I thought you were my friend! But you have . . .

_____

_____

_____

Your friend, David

4 Match the following Scripture verses with the statements in the right-hand column:

Matthew 5:24   You should be willing to forgive your friends over and over.
Matthew 18:15   Be a devoted friend, hold your friends in high honor.
Matthew 18:21-22   Don't slander or speak against a friend.
Romans 12:10   Settle matters quickly when you are at odds with someone.
Romans 14:21   If a friend wrongs you, talk about it and try to win him or her back.
James 4:11   Don't ignore a friend who needs something you can give.
1 John 3:17   Don't do anything to cause a friend to fall.

5 Pick one thing you will do to be a really good friend. Write it below:

Friendship Pledge:

_____

_____

WHAT A PAL!

Topic: Loyalty.
Biblical Basis: Psalm 55

Purpose of this Session:

Sooner or later, every young person will be hurt by a friend because of shifting loyalties, confused priorities, or selfish interests. This TalkSheet will help your group understand that good friends do their best to remain loyal.

To Introduce the Topic:

Let your students talk about physical wounds. Call on volunteers to describe injuries they have suffered. What's the worst pain they ever experienced? Point out that one of the worst wounds of all is not really a physical injury, but the pain of a heart broken by the betrayal of a friend. Another idea is to describe or show various healing aids such as bandages, elastic bandages, a crutch, and so on. Have students explain what sort of injury each item is used for. Then discuss the pain of a friend's betrayal.

The Discussion:

Item #1: Have a few willing students share their results. Take a vote to see if your students feel problems such as these are common among young people. Say, "We all agree that it would be best if these things never happened among friends. I'm hoping that, as we go over these things, you will decide in your hearts to be the best friends you can be."

Item #2: Give students a few moments to share and discuss. Jot ideas on the chalkboard.

Item #3: Have several students share what they read, until a good understanding of the passage is obtained. Ask if anyone is surprised that someone like King David would have problems with friends who betray.

Item #4: If time is short, assign a few passages each to smaller groups. The passages will support many of the things your students have just said. Ask students to give concrete examples of each passage (e.g., "I had to forgive a friend who repeated gossip without asking me if it were true").

   Students may say something like, "I tried to talk to my friend about the problem, but he just turned away and wouldn't say anything. What do I do?" Refer them to Romans 12:18: "If it is possible, as far as it depends on you, live in peace with everyone." Do what you can, then leave it up to God.

Item #5: Allow students to share their pledges. Encourage them to hang onto them in a wallet or a purse to serve as a reminder of true friendship.

To Close the Session:

Encourage your students to consider you their friend. Make a "Friendship Pledge" to them to be available and supportive, to continue to pray for them, and to work to make your times together beneficial.

Outside Activities:

1. Assemble students into pairs or threes—boys with boys, girls with girls—to do friendly things together for a week (phone each other, shop, eat). Try to match people who aren't well acquainted but compatible. Have students report on the results next week.

2. Get adult volunteers to spend a Sunday with your kids, with a ratio of one adult to one young person if possible. After attending church together, they can go out for lunch or other entertainment. This is best done in small groups so no student feels intimidated being alone with an unfamiliar adult.

DOWN AND OUT

1 Why do you think people are down and out? (Check all that apply.)

___ They are victims of society
___ They are lazy
___ They are paying the price for not working hard in school
___ They are addicts or alcoholics
___ They are mentally unstable
___ They are unlucky
___ They are being punished for doing something wrong
___ They made a series of bad choices
___ They are victims of unfortunate circumstances
___ They are born that way

2 If you were approached by a stranger who wanted a handout, what would you do? _____
_____

If you found yourself on the street without food or money, would you beg from people?
Yes__ No__ Why or why not?

3 Read Psalm 82:2-4. What portion of this passage best matches the descriptions given below?
A boy comes from a divorced home. His dad is never around.

A boy is a klutz in sports. Nobody want him on their team. Everyone laughs at him.

A kid has moved here from a third world country. Five members of her family live in a
one-bedroom apartment. She buys her clothes at second-hand stores.

A boy is picked on for his speech impediment. People imitate him and laugh at him.

4 When you see a person who is weak, needy, defenseless, or hurting in some other way and is being
given a hard time by other kids, what do you tend to do? (Circle all that usually apply.)

Watch	**Feel Bad**	**Say Something**	**Say Nothing**
Defend	**Join In**	**Walk Away**	**Pray**
Tell Someone	**Comfort**	**Laugh**	**Feel Nothing**

5 Suppose there is a kid at your school who is unpopular because he or she looks or dresses oddly.
What could you do to help this kid?

DOWN AND OUT

Topic: Helping the needy.
Biblical Basis: Psalm 82

Purpose of this Session:

The down and out are everywhere. Most of us think of them as the homeless, the street people, and the slum dwellers. But these are only one facet of needy people. The down and out are walking around in every suburb and on every campus. They are the kids who feel rejected. The kids crying out for a father or mother to love them. The oddballs, misfits, and others who don't fit with their peers. This TalkSheet will help your kids to recognize that they have an obligation to help, in some way, people the world would cast away.

To Introduce the Topic:

Select two groups of kids, with four or five in each group. Have the groups assemble at the far end of the room, and tell them that their goal is to get to the other side of the room first. There's only one problem. One member in each group cannot use any portion of the body except one arm. These people cannot walk or crawl, but they may drag themselves by one arm if they like. Give your students no other rules or time to think about how they will get their whole group over to the other side. Obviously, the best way to get the whole team across is for the "handicapped" member to be carried by his or her teammates. Follow up this exercise by explaining that there are people who sometimes need the help of others, and that those of us who will carry those people for a way will end up being winners in life.

The Discussion:

Item #1: Discuss the reasons your kids think people become down and out. Talk about the various causes for various situations. Allow for disagreement.

Item #2: Have several kids share their answers. Ask your kids how they would get food and shelter if they found themselves in need.

Item #3: Explore the teaching of the psalm about our duty to the poor, the helpless, and the needy. Talk about how people who are well fed and housed can also be weak, oppressed, or needy (for example, a kid without friends is socially needy).

Item #4: Discuss our reactions to people who are down and out, unpopular, or being picked on. Talk about what we should or could do in those instances.

Item #5: Have your group brainstorm ways they could defend or help those at their schools who are needy or hurting in some way. Encourage them to think of real people at their schools who might need their help.

To Close the Session:

Encourage your students to take seriously the obligation to help those who are in some way suffering, hurting, or in need. Remind them that this is not just a Skid Row problem. Many needs are not as visible as a smelly, ragged panhandler might present. Challenge kids to not merely feel bad when someone is picked on for no good reason, but to have the courage to get involved in making that person feel better and to show the love of Christ to them.

Outside Activity:

Arrange with a local rescue mission, old folks home, homeless shelter, or facility for disabled children to have your group come and provide a meal or other services to their clientele.

Praise GOD From Whom All Blessings Flow

1 Circle which one of these things you would most like to have happen to you:

People write hit songs about you
People form a fan club for you

People write books about you
People give you priceless gifts
People build a museum in your honor

2 Read Psalm 96. Fill in the blanks on this short paraphrased version:

Verse 1— "_____ to the Lord a new _____."
Verse 3— "_____ his glory among the nations."
Verse 8— "Bring an _____ and come into his courts."
Verse 9— "_____ the Lord in the in the splendor of his_____."
Verse 11— "Let the heavens _____, let the earth be _____."

3 Rate yourself! Where do you see yourself fitting into the following areas?

	No Way	Maybe	Yes, That's Me
Singing before the youth group	☐	☐	☐
Telling others about God	☐	☐	☐
Giving money to God's work	☐	☐	☐
Worshipping God	☐	☐	☐
Rejoicing because I'm a Christian	☐	☐	☐

4 Maybe you can't write a hit song or a book about God, but there are some things you can do! Pick one or two from this list:

Music
Put together a band to play a cool Christian song.
Write a simple Christian song.
Sing in church if you have a good voice.
Bring a cool Christian CD to play.

Telling Others
Invite a friend to the next youth event.
Tell someone why you're a Christian.
Help plan a fun event where kids can hear about Jesus.

Gifts to God
Plan a fund-raiser for a Christian cause.
Sell some of your possessions and give the money to the youth fund.

Worship
Make a poster for class that lists fifteen great things about God.
Write a prayer that tells ten reasons why you love God.

Joyful Imitation
Memorize a Bible passage—and do what it says.

5 Is there some way you can PRAISE God this week? Pick one letter from the word PRAISE below and use it in a phrase, telling what you will do. (Here are some examples: **P**—I will **P**ray every morning; **R**—I will contribute some of my **R**iches to the youth fund; **A**—I will bring **A** Christian CD . . . You get the idea!)

P
R
A
I
S
E

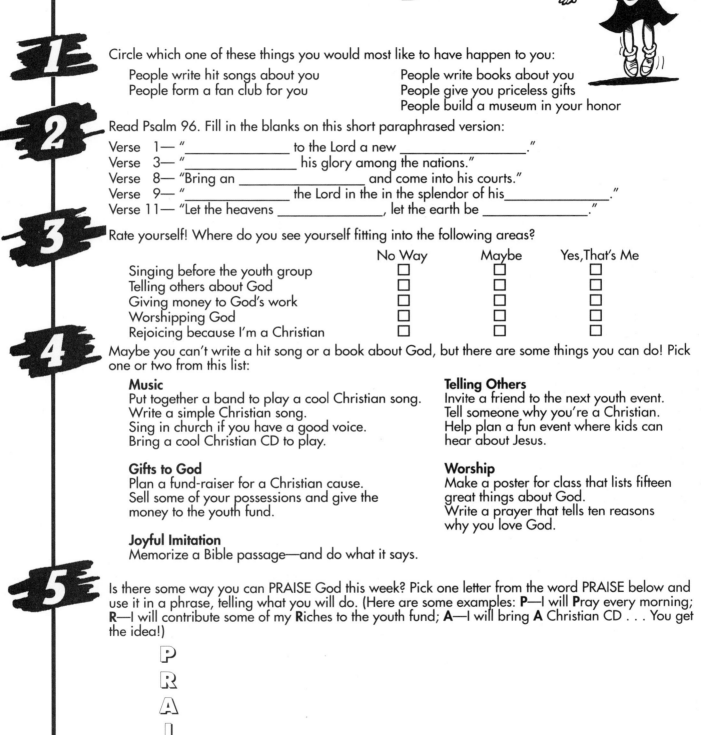

Date Used_____ Group_____

PRAISE GOD FROM WHOM ALL BLESSINGS FLOW

Topic: Glorifying God.
Biblical Basis: Psalm 96

Purpose of this Session:

The greatest confessions of faith throughout the church age all say that the chief end of man is to glorify God. Psalm 96 gives a list of five ways to do so: Sing praise to the Lord; tell others of his glory; give him your best; worship him; live a life of joyful holiness. Use this TalkSheet to teach your students specific things they can do to glorify God.

To Introduce the Topic:

Tell your kids how the ancient Canaanites used to "glorify" their gods. In those days, a family that bought or built a new house would dedicate it to the gods. To do so, they would sacrifice one of their children and put his or her remains in an urn in the main room! Imagine the proud parents at the housewarming party! (You might ask how many kids in the class would be dead if it was still the custom to sacrifice the firstborn.)

Say, "Happily, things aren't like that with almighty God. But how does God want to be glorified and celebrated by us? Let's find out."

The Discussion:

Item #1: Let volunteers say what they picked and why. Explain that these things, which sound wildly improbable, are actually the sort of things people have done throughout history to worship God. The great hymns of the faith, the books of the Bible, the untold self-sacrifices and uncountable dollars given by believers, the shrines, and the "fan club" of the faithful who have tried to imitate Jesus Christ all over the earth—these are to God's glory.

Item #2: Help your students understand that Psalm 96 commands believers to glorify God by singing a new song (verse 1), declaring his glory (verse 3), giving gifts to him (verse 8), worshipping him, and imitating his holiness (verse 9)—and doing all this joyfully (verse 11).

Item #3: Chances are, your students will rate themselves low in most or all of these areas. Tell them that's OK, because the next item will help them to see that there are fun ways for them to glorify God.

Item #4: If you do not plan to do the Outside Activity, discuss some of the things students have picked from the list. Point out that each person in class should be able to find at least one thing to do on the list. Tell them that God is truly glorified when young people do things like these.

If you choose to do the Outside Activity, now is a good time to set a date and start the ball rolling.

Item #5: Let volunteers share their ideas.

To Close the Session:

This is a good opportunity to remind your learners of two things. First, God is great and worthy to be praised. Second, the first step of true worship—one that brings real glory to him—is the step of turning one's life over to God. If you have some non-Christians in your class, allow a quiet time for them to prayerfully consider receiving Jesus as Savior.

Outside Activity:

Plan a worship service for your next class time (or talk to your minister about a church worship service led by the youth). The service could include posters, the reciting of memorized Scriptures, announcements regarding planned fund-raisers and fun events, live music (if any), recorded music, prayers and the like. Everyone can have a part.

HEAVY DUTY LOVE

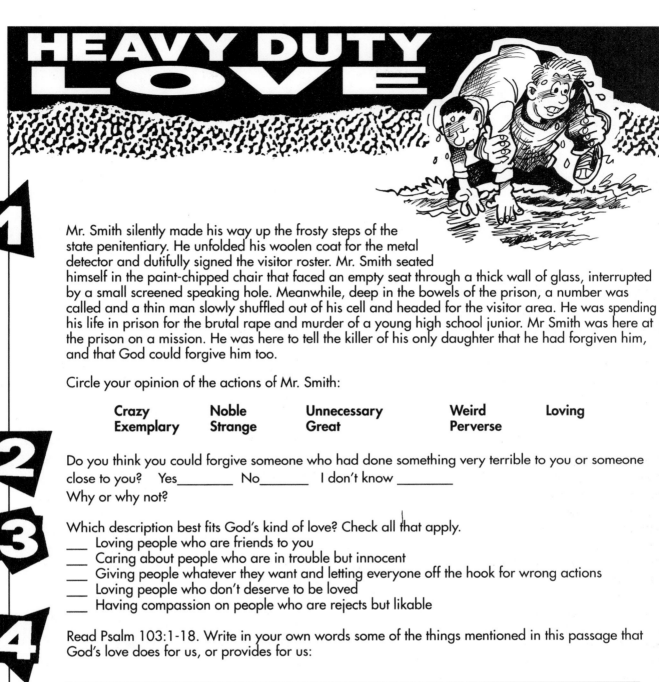

1 Mr. Smith silently made his way up the frosty steps of the state penitentiary. He unfolded his woolen coat for the metal detector and dutifully signed the visitor roster. Mr. Smith seated himself in the paint-chipped chair that faced an empty seat through a thick wall of glass, interrupted by a small screened speaking hole. Meanwhile, deep in the bowels of the prison, a number was called and a thin man slowly shuffled out of his cell and headed for the visitor area. He was spending his life in prison for the brutal rape and murder of a young high school junior. Mr Smith was here at the prison on a mission. He was here to tell the killer of his only daughter that he had forgiven him, and that God could forgive him too.

Circle your opinion of the actions of Mr. Smith:

Crazy   **Noble**   **Unnecessary**   **Weird**   **Loving**
Exemplary   **Strange**   **Great**   **Perverse**

2 Do you think you could forgive someone who had done something very terrible to you or someone close to you? Yes_____ No_____ I don't know _____
Why or why not?

3 Which description best fits God's kind of love? Check all that apply.
___ Loving people who are friends to you
___ Caring about people who are in trouble but innocent
___ Giving people whatever they want and letting everyone off the hook for wrong actions
___ Loving people who don't deserve to be loved
___ Having compassion on people who are rejects but likable

4 Read Psalm 103:1-18. Write in your own words some of the things mentioned in this passage that God's love does for us, or provides for us:

_____

_____

_____

5 If you were going to try to imitate God's kind of love, which of the following things would you do? (Check all that apply.)
___ Stand up for those being put down
___ Walk around acting religious and holy
___ Give people hugs and act all mushy
___ Control my temper so that I am slow to get angry
___ Lecture those who are doing wrong things
___ Forget about paying back those who have harmed me
___ Forgive wrongs done toward me
___ Make people fear me cause God is my Father

HEAVY DUTY LOVE

Topic: God's kind of love.
Biblical Basis: Psalm 103

Purpose of this Session:

Agape love is the highest form of loving expression. This is the kind of love displayed by God—pure, self-giving, rare, heavy duty love. Kids can discover this kind of love and can begin to display it in their lives. This TalkSheet introduces this kind of love to your kids and encourages them to see how God might show his love through them.

To Introduce the Topic:

Demonstrate the various and insignificant meanings that we have for the word love as a lead-in to today's topic. Ask kids to complete the sentence, "I love . . . " List their answers on a chalkboard. Discuss the difference between loving ice cream and loving our parents.

The Discussion:

Item #1: Discuss the case of Mr. Smith and his forgiveness of the person who murdered his daughter. Discuss what kind of amazing love a person would have to have in order to offer this kind of forgiveness.
Item #2: Have your students elaborate on their answers. Why would they respond the way they've indicated?
Item #3: Discuss the nature of God's kind of love. Introduce the idea of *agape* love—love that loves people even if they don't deserve it. Talk about who best demonstrated this kind of love for us.
Item #4: Explore the fantastic promises from this psalm. Ask your kids to brainstorm modern-day examples of this kind of divine love. Discuss what each one means for us.
Item #5: Discuss what kind of behavior copies godly love. Contrast *agape* love with merely being nice to people who like you, from whom you need a favor, or you are trying to impress.

To Close the Session:

Summarize the ideas about godly love that have been brought up during the TalkSheet discussion. Point out that it is God's desire for each of us to begin to display this kind of love for one another. By having the Holy Spirit dwelling in us, we can actually have the power to love people in the same way God does.

Outside Activity:

Ask your students to think of a person they know who needs heavy duty love, or who it would take heavy duty love to treat kindly. Ask your students to commit themselves to pray every day this week for this person as the first step in acting lovingly towards him or her. Encourage kids to look for at least one action or word they can do for or say to this person this next week that might come from the heart of God.

NO FEAR

1 Which of the following would cause you the most fear?

_____ Walking a tightrope across Niagara Falls
_____ Falling into a den of black widow spiders
_____ Being held hostage by an insane terrorist
_____ Being on a sinking ship in the middle of the ocean
_____ Seeing a great white shark swim under you while you are snorkeling
_____ Bringing home a failing report card
_____ Seeing an intruder in your room when you awake in the middle of the night
_____ Falling into an open grave during a midnight shortcut through the cemetery
_____ Being thrown out of the gym naked as the school assembles on the playing field for a fire drill

2 Describe a time that you were *really* fearful:

3 Which of the following fears do you think are the most common, with #1 being the most common?

_____ The fear of having no friends
_____ The fear of being beaten up by a bully
_____ The fear of being rejected by people
_____ The fear of being thought of as ugly
_____ The fear that your parents will divorce
_____ The fear that you will get caught doing wrong things
_____ The fear that no one will care about you one way or the other

4 Read Psalm 112:1-10. Put a star next to any of the common fears listed above that would vanish by being like the person talked about in this passage.

5 What kind of prescription would you write for a person who is fearful about how others think of him or her?

Rx

NO FEAR

Topic: Getting free from fear.
Biblical Basis: Psalm 112

Purpose of this Session:

Sooner or later, fear gets to us all. It may not be the terror of things that go bump in the night or a phobia about spiders, but it could well be the fear of not being accepted or failing at school. Many kids are often fearful of how they are viewed by their peers. Some are fearful that they will be seen as a coward or a nerd, others that they will be thought of as unattractive or a loser. This psalm offers a great prescription for kids or adults who agonize internally about common fears: Trust in and obedience to God can wipe them out.

To Introduce the Topic:

Divide the room into three parts. Give each section a name: *AIDS, Nuclear War,* and *Severe Acne.* Next, ask your kids to go to the section of the room that represents what people fear most. Then ask them to go to the section that represents what kids their age might fear most. Finally, ask them to go to the section that represents something that is most likely to happen to at least one of their friends before they get out of high school. Use this as a lead-in to talk about personal fears.

The Discussion:

Item #1: Talk about the things that would cause each person the most fear. Note that some will be more afraid of heights than of things that go bump in the night. Some may be more afraid of the consequences of bad grades than perishing in the middle of the ocean.

Item #2: Have a few volunteers share their answers. If you have a large group or are limited on time, break your students into pairs or threes and have them share their stories with one another.

Item #3: Discuss fears that are common rather than exceptional. Discuss the way that these kind of fears are different than fears that bring raw terror. Point out that everyone knows that these fears exist, but few people will discuss or acknowledge them as fears. Why is that? Have a few volunteers share their answers.

Item #4: Talk about the fears that might be relieved by following the advice in the Bible. Talk about how these fears are eliminated by God.

Item #5: Ask your kids to prescribe advice based on Psalm 112 for any of their friends who might be having a hard time with the most common fears. Have several volunteers share their answers.

To Close the Session:

Encourage your students to take seriously the fact that God wants to drive away fears from their lives. Challenge them to bring their lives into line with the teaching of Scripture. Stress that everyone has hidden fears that God can and will put to rest if we let him. Having those fears does not mean that we are cowards, but that we are normal human beings.

Outside Activity:

Have a contest for your kids to make a T-shirt design (based on concept rather than quality of art) that expresses the idea that a relationship with God dissolves our fears. Take the concept to a person who will turn it into final art, and have T-shirts made for your kids.

PRAISE THE LORD

1 What do you think it means when someone says, "Praise the Lord"? (Check all that apply.)

___ Three cheers for God
___ An expression used by "religious" folk
___ A spiritual "Oh Boy!"
___ Look at me, I'm spiritual
___ Thanks, God!
___ Yay!
___ God is awesome to me
___ Something you should say even if you don't know why

2 What percentage of people do you think *really* praise God? Place an X on the line to mark your answer.

0%-- 100%

3 Read Psalm 113, and then fill in the following blanks:

Let the _____ of the Lord be praised
The Lord is to be praised both _____ and _____
The Lord is _____ over all the nations
His glory is _____ the heavens
He _____ the poor and needy from the dust and sits them with _____
He makes the childless woman a _____ _____

4 It is one thing to praise God for what he has done, it is another thing to praise God for who he is and what he is like. Describe in your own words some of the awesome ways that God is.
God is:

5 Complete these sentences:

When I think of what God is like and compare it to what I am like, I feel . . .

When I think about what God is like, it makes me want to . . .

PRAISE THE LORD!

Topic: Giving God praise.
Biblical Basis: Psalm 113

Purpose of this Session:

God is worthy of praise. We may thank him from time to time, and we come to him with our requests and emergencies; but few of us truly praise him for simply being who he is. The habit of praising God is a great one for young teens to learn. In praising God for who he is and what he is like, we are forced out of our self-obsession and into a mode of thinking that quickly humbles us as we measure ourselves against the Creator. This TalkSheet will help kids to realize that respecting a power far greater than ourselves will bring us closer to that power. Kids will see that praising God is not just a frivolous expression, but an act of worship.

To Introduce the Topic:

Select one good-natured student from your group and stand him or her in front of the others. Ask your students to help you create a "praise list" for this person, listing everything about him or her that is noteworthy. Be prepared for humor and silliness. List everything suggested from "He has clean nails" to "She really cares for others." Note that in order to praise your student, it was necessary to observe things about him or her and to put a bit of thought into the subject. Let your students know that while it can be fun to praise a friend, there is one person with whom praise is serious business.

The Discussion:

Item #1: Talk about what it really means to praise the Lord—to acknowledge him for who he is and revere him as the Lord. Discuss why the expression might lose its meaning with careless use.
Item #2: Discuss why we tend not to put much time or effort into giving God praise. Ask your students what they think keeps people from praising God (thinking we are self-sufficient, feeling like we're OK on our own, etc.).
Item #3: Point out that the writer of Psalm 113 praises God for both who he is as well as what he can and will do for humans.
Item #4: Help your kids to focus on the attributes of God. Read Psalm 8 and list the attributes described there on a chalkboard.
Item #5: Discuss the idea that praising God reminds us of our own smallness and of our need for and appreciation of him. Talk about what kind of behavior changes can occur once we see ourselves as we really are in comparison with the might of God.

To Close the Session:

Close by singing together a chorus or song that tells of God's power and awesomeness, such as "Our God is an Awesome God" or "The Battle Belongs to the Lord." If you are not familiar with any songs, ask the musicians around your church to give you some ideas. (Another option is to play a recorded version of a quality praise song.)

Outside Activity:

Have your students commit themselves to taking time to praise God every day for a week. Ask them to keep a journal of what they praised God for each day. Have them bring the journals to the next meeting; at that time, have a few volunteers share what they thought and did.

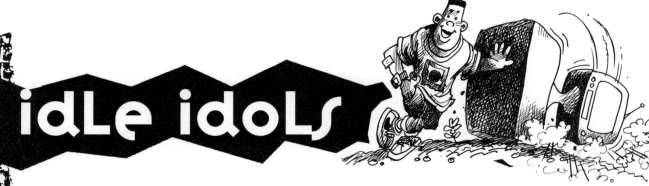

idLe idoLs

1 Do you think modern people worship "idols" today? **Yes**_____ **No** _____

2 Circle the phrase that best describes the idea of worship:

Bowing down and groveling in front of an image
Going to some kind of religious service
Singing real loud with your arms up and eyes closed
Honoring, caring about, obeying, and putting first someone or something
Sacrificing hard-earned money and time
Putting pictures of the object or person you worship all around your room

3 Read Psalm 115:2-8. See if you can find the "curse" described in this passage upon all who worship false gods (hint: It's in verse 8). Write your version of the curse below:

4 What are some things that kids might worship or place before the real God?

5 There is an old saying that goes, "God is not God at all unless he is God over all."
Do you:

Agree_____ or **Disagree** _____ with this statement?
Why?

6 Read the following verses and describe in your own words what they mean to you:

Exodus 20:3-4 _____

Matthew 22:37 _____

Matthew 6:21 _____

IDLE IDOLS

Topic: Putting God first.
Biblical Basis: Psalm 115
Purpose of this Session:

Worshipping an idol is the last thing most kids think they might be guilty of. It is a supremely primitive act. It is also a very modern one. Technology has not eliminated idols; it has merely replaced them with sleeker, shinier, and more sophisticated models.

Kids are surrounded by idols that compete for their worship, yet they are usually not even aware of it. Some of the modern idols are made of metal and plastic. Other idols can include the desire to be popular and the ambition to succeed.

Idols often have the trademarks of something good. A person who is so focused on getting good grades in school that he or she neglects time with God is in danger of making grades an idol. In short, an idol is anything that comes before God. Many of us are far deeper into worshipping idols than we ever imagined. Use this TalkSheet to bring these ideas home!

To Introduce the Topic:

Hand out paper and pencils. Ask your kids to draw a picture of an idol. Tell them to give it a name and describe what supposed power it has. Encourage your students to have some fun with this project. For example, an idol could be called the Grade Goddess; it could have power over passing and failing any class. Share the silly idols that have been created, then discuss the fact that anyone who seriously worshipped any of the idols made in the class would be a fool and a laughingstock. Lead into the first TalkSheet question from this point.

The Discussion:

Item #1: Discuss whether or not people worship idols today. Discuss what some candidates for modern-day idols might be.

Item #2: Talk about what it means to worship something or someone. Ask kids to define the meaning of the term based on the ideas given. Discuss whether a person can worship something that is not alive.

Item #3: Help your students locate the description of people who worship an idol in Psalm 115:8—they become just as spiritually dead, unfeeling, and blind as the object they worship. Discuss the difference between what happens to idolators and what happens to those who put God first in their lives.

Item #4: Discuss what things are likely to challenge God for lordship in our lives. List what is suggested on a chalkboard. Note that many of the things mentioned are not bad in and of themselves, but only when they are put ahead of God.

Item #5: Have a few volunteers share their answers. Reinforce the idea that whatever is first in our life is truly our god.

Item #6: Help your kids to develop responses to those passages that are specific to their daily lives. Encourage them to articulate what these passages are saying to them as modern-day teenagers.

To Close the Session:

Once again, hand out pencils and paper. This time, ask kids to create a picture of things that might become idols in their lives if not held in check. Allow any kids who are willing to share their drawings and talk about what strives for first place in their lives. Finally, have your kids destroy their papers as a symbolic act of their desire to have God as Lord over all of their lives.

Outside Activity:

Create a follow-up questionnaire to today's lesson and drop it in the mail a few days after you've done this TalkSheet. Ask kids to do a self-evaluation to see if they have put their actions behind their words as far as making God the number-one priority in their lives.

SOUL POLLUTION

1 The following items can pollute a person's thinking or negatively affect his or her relationship with God. List them in order of their potential for harm, with #1 being the most harmful:

___MTV   ___Nudie magazines   ___TV   ___Radio
___Newspapers   ___Gambling   ___R-rated movies   ___Music with
___Glamour magazines ___Comic books   ___Video games   foul lyrics
___Tabloid TV shows ___*Sports Illustrated*'s ___PG-13 movies   ___X-rated
___Soap operas   swimsuit issue   ___Talk shows   movies
___Other:

2 Who do you think should decide what is "soul pollution" for you?
___Parents   ___Church leaders   ___Teachers   ___Friends   ___Yourself

Why?

3 How do you feel after immersing yourself in a puddle of soul pollution? (Circle one)

Peaceful   **Guilty**   **Happy**   **Fulfilled**   **Ashamed**
Excited   **Embarrassed**   **Weak**   **Joyful**   **Proud**

4 Read Psalm 119:9-11. Describe in your own words:
What was the question asked?_____
What was the solution? _____

5 Jim is a Christian. He is also a typical kid who likes to watch MTV, listen to popular music, and go to movies that all of his friends rave about. The problem is, sometimes Jim comes away from a movie feeling "dirty" and far from God. The same thing happens from time to time after watching MTV or listening to certain songs. Jim's youth director once said that Christians shouldn't watch or listen to anything that they wouldn't watch or listen to if Jesus was hanging out with them.

Jim doesn't want to become a hermit, yet he doesn't like the feeling he gets when he tries to enjoy what is popular with his friends. What should Jim do?

SOUL POLLUTION

Topic: Keeping a pure heart.
Biblical Basis: Psalm 119:9-11

Purpose of this Session:

The world is like dirt—it is hard to play around in it too long without becoming stained. Kids who get one or two hours a week of spiritual input are bombarded the rest of their waking hours with messages that are often in total opposition to those values. Pollution of the soul is the result.

The psalm writer saw the same problem in his day. He asks, "How can a young man keep his way pure?" The solution given serves as a set of filters to block the debris of sin: living according to God's Word, seeking God with all the heart, and committing God's Word to memory.

Kids who focus on Christ will find themselves losing their taste for the offerings of the world, and more quickly able to sense the foul odor of soul pollution. While it is unrealistic to expect that kids can avoid *all* soul pollution, they can learn to be selective and careful about what they allow into their minds and hearts.

To Introduce the Topic:

Talk about stuff that you and your kids have found in food that did not belong there. Be prepared for some stomach-churning stories about bits of hair, fingernails, rubbish, and much more packed into a meal. Talk about their responses to these delicacies. Did your students go ahead and consume the food? Did they make a stink? Discuss how we are often far more careful to screen what we are putting into our bodies than what we are putting into our minds.

The Discussion:

Item #1: Discuss the various means by which soul pollution reaches us. Find out what items kids perceive to have the most potential for damage.
Item #2: Discuss the role of parents, church leaders, teachers, and other adults in giving direction and wisdom in the choices to be made.
Item #3: Explore the results of overexposure to soul pollution. Talk about the toxic effect it can have on our relationship with God. Share an example from your own life when you were overexposed to soul pollution, then have a few willing students share their examples.
Item #4: Identify the solutions offered in Psalm 119:9-11 to a young person seeking purity: living according to God's Word, seeking God with all our heart, obeying his commands, storing God's Word in our heart (memorizing Scripture), and striving to avoid sin. Discuss how we can incorporate these principles into our everyday lives. Encourage students to offer specific examples.
Item #5: Discuss possible solutions to the problem that Jim is having. Talk about the need to be self-monitoring and discerning about what we see, hear, read, and do. Discuss the liberty that a person has as a Christian and the need to make wise choices.

To Close the Session:

Help students to see that they have a responsibility to keep their heart and soul free from pollution and ungodly influences. Let them know that this does not mean that everything in the secular world is off-limits, but that they must develop the wisdom to know what has the potential to pollute their souls. Help them see that not everything that the popular culture embraces is worth their investment.

Outside Activity:

Invite your students to create their own Soul Pollution Rating System for movies, TV shows, and musical recordings. Tell them to base their evaluations on the aspects of these products that are the most detrimental to their spiritual growth.

A Wasted Life

1 Put a check next to any of the following that seem to you to be a waste of time:

___ Watching TV all day   ___ Exploring uncharted places

___ Selling ice cubes to Alaskans   ___ Becoming a missionary

___ Becoming a brain surgeon   ___ Becoming a criminal

___ Being paralyzed   ___ Being a drug addict

___ Being a scientist   ___ Going to war

___ Being a playboy   ___ Chasing after romance all the time

2 What makes a life valuable? What makes a life wasted?

Valuable:_____

Wasted:_____

3 Read Psalm 127:1 and Matthew 7:24-27. Then answer the following questions:

a. What does the house in these verses represent?_____

b. What does the rock represent? _____

c. What does the sand represent? _____

d. What is the end result from building your "house" while ignoring the advice of the Master Builder?_____

4 List some things you could do with your life that would make it valuable:

5 Which of these ideas do you think are true, and which do you think are false?

___Most people in the world live a wasted life

___All people have the potential for a meaningful life

___ Most people in the world live a valuable life

___ Many people who claim to be Christians live a wasteful life

Why did you answer the way you did?

A WASTED LIFE

Topic: Making our lives count.
Biblical Basis: Psalm 127

Purpose of this Session:

The students in your group have most of their lives in front of them. They still can reach the goals and dreams they aspire to; they can invest in things that will enrich their lives in the future and pay off in the present. But any life can be misspent and wasted. Not every investment pays off positively. The only way to invest a life so that it has meaning and purpose is to place it in God's hands. This TalkSheet will underscore the need to wisely construct our lives according to the will of God in order to live a life that is not squandered on crumbling things.

To Introduce the Topic:

Divide the room in two parts. Make one side the *Agree* side and the other the *Disagree* side. Tell your students, "There is a saying that says, 'The greatest sin a person can commit is that of a wasted life'." Have the kids move to the side of the room that indicates how they feel about this statement. When everyone has moved, have a few willing students share why they chose their answers.

The Discussion:

Item #1: Discuss which activities your kids consider a waste of time and which activities they think are profitable ways to live. Invite them to add other things to this list.
Item #2: Discuss what it takes to make a life valuable and what wastes a life. Note that lives with value seem to be concerned with things outside of mere self-interest.
Item #3: Help your students to answer these questions (the house stands for our lives; the rock represents the foundation of the words of Christ; the sand stands for the lack of foundation in those who ignore Christ's words). Remind them that a life lived outside of God's plan is headed for a wet and slippery end.
Item #4: Have kids share specific things that they could do to give their lives eternal value and meaning. Help kids think of practical ideas such as telling a friend about Christ, showing love towards a person that others ignore, and creating a piece of art that reflects God's beauty. (Explain that while the art will not last forever, the act of worship that motivated it will).
Item #5: Discuss the fact that most people are living lives void of eternal meaning and purpose—a "vain" life as the psalmist puts it—because they do not allow God to be the one who calls the shots in their lives. Point out that this is true for many Christians as well. Challenge your kids to invest their time and energy into following God's way for their lives.

To Close the Session:

Pass out paper and pencils. Tell your students that when people die, it is common for newspapers to run an obituary telling about the person and listing their accomplishments. Ask your students to imagine that there is a similar kind of announcement in heaven—only instead of communicating who has departed, it announces who is arriving and what they have accomplished of eternal value on earth. Ask you students to write down what they would like to have announced about them as *they* enter the "pearly gates."

Outside Activity:

Collect the names and addresses of people who are leading lives rich in meaning and the guidance of God. Invite each student to write at least one of these people a short letter asking the person about his or her life, how he or she has been able to stay on track with God's plan, and what advice he or she has to help the young writer plot an equally worthwhile course.

well made

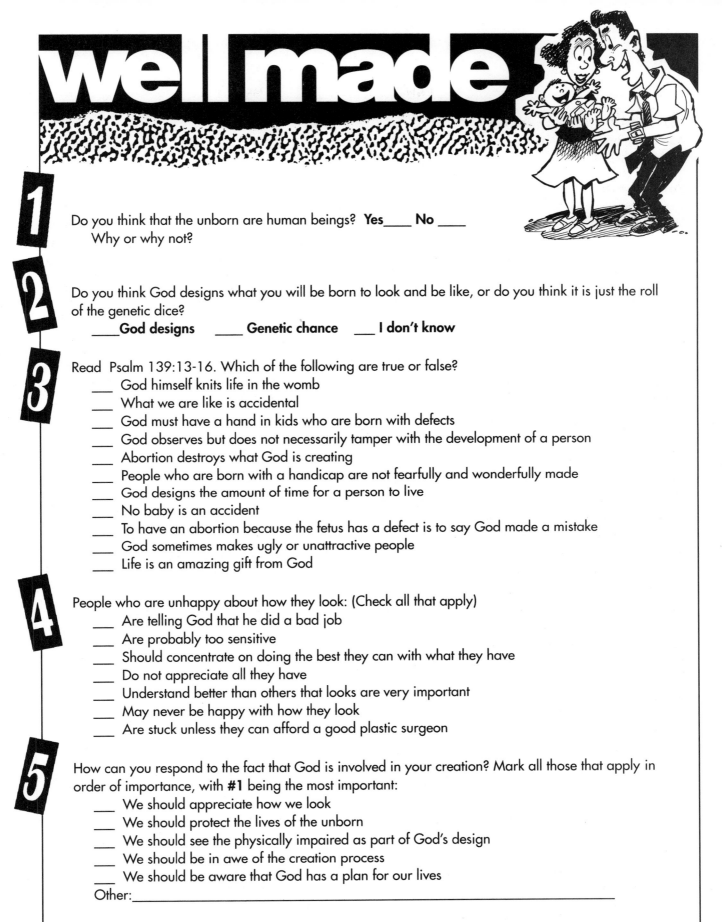

1 Do you think that the unborn are human beings? **Yes____ No ____**
   Why or why not?

2 Do you think God designs what you will be born to look and be like, or do you think it is just the roll of the genetic dice?
   ____**God designs** ____ **Genetic chance** ___ **I don't know**

3 Read Psalm 139:13-16. Which of the following are true or false?
   ___ God himself knits life in the womb
   ___ What we are like is accidental
   ___ God must have a hand in kids who are born with defects
   ___ God observes but does not necessarily tamper with the development of a person
   ___ Abortion destroys what God is creating
   ___ People who are born with a handicap are not fearfully and wonderfully made
   ___ God designs the amount of time for a person to live
   ___ No baby is an accident
   ___ To have an abortion because the fetus has a defect is to say God made a mistake
   ___ God sometimes makes ugly or unattractive people
   ___ Life is an amazing gift from God

4 People who are unhappy about how they look: (Check all that apply)
   ___ Are telling God that he did a bad job
   ___ Are probably too sensitive
   ___ Should concentrate on doing the best they can with what they have
   ___ Do not appreciate all they have
   ___ Understand better than others that looks are very important
   ___ May never be happy with how they look
   ___ Are stuck unless they can afford a good plastic surgeon

5 How can you respond to the fact that God is involved in your creation? Mark all those that apply in order of importance, with **#1** being the most important:
   ___ We should appreciate how we look
   ___ We should protect the lives of the unborn
   ___ We should see the physically impaired as part of God's design
   ___ We should be in awe of the creation process
   ___ We should be aware that God has a plan for our lives
   Other:_____

WELL MADE

Topic: The holiness of human life.
Biblical Basis: Psalm 139:13-16

Purpose of this Session:

Kids have heard the phrase, "All men [persons] are created equal." Most of them do not believe it to be true. All they have to do is to look around them and see that some people are far less equal than others. There are kids who are beautiful or handsome, and some who are homely. There are those who are mentally or physically gifted, and those who operate under a handicap.

This TalkSheet explores the truth that God has his hand on our lives from the moment of conception. It is he who brings, develops, and sustains life. It is he who allows the assembly of genes that gives one a large nose and another acne. God is involved in the creation process of every human being. His direct acts of creation make the idea of abortion a reprehensible problem for most Christians. His plan for each life starts at conception and his plan is good.

To Introduce the Topic:

On a chalkboard write: **Physical**, **Mind**, and **Talent**. Ask your kids to describe anyone they know or know of who excels in any one of these three areas. Talk about child prodigies like Mozart (who was writing symphonies at age seven). Ask your students to come up with some ideas as to why these people can do what they can do. Let your kids know that this session will explore the idea that God, from the very start, designs not only these people with exceptional skills, but average and specially-challenged people as well.

The Discussion:

Item #1: Allow your students to freely discuss whether they think the unborn are truly human, or at what point the unborn become human. Don't close off the discussion with a definitive answer; let the debate rage.

Item #2: Talk about how God and genetics may work together to create each individual human being. If you have time, discuss the issue of humans engineering the genetics of another person.

Item #3: After reading the psalm, discuss the ideas that are found there. Help kids to apply these truths to their own creation and the creation of others who have different capabilities than they do. Be prepared for disagreement.

Item #4: Discuss how people should think and feel about their own looks. Give examples of people who are attractive for other reasons besides their looks, and people who are ugly in spite of their external attractiveness.

Item #5: Have your students share which idea from this psalm has the most impact on how they view human life. Encourage kids to appreciate how God has made them; at the same time, allow for less-than-enthusiastic responses from students who are struggling with their perceived inadequacies.

To Close the Session:

Pass out pencils and paper. Have each of your students write a thank-you note to God for what he has given them not only in the area of physical looks but also in personality and talents.

Ask a few willing students to read their letters aloud.

Outside Activity:

Invite a person who was born with a special challenge to come and talk to your students about why he or she feels he or she is "fearfully and wonderfully made," and how the person has learned to cope with the challenges he or she faces.

DRY INSIDE

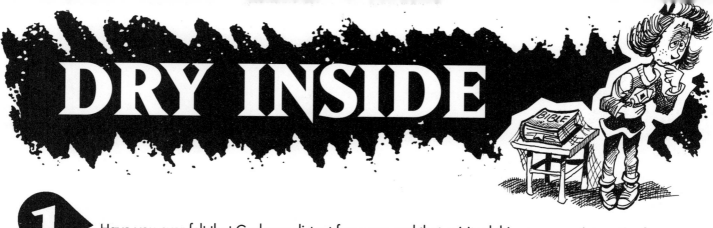

1 Have you ever felt that God was distant from you and that spiritual things were uninteresting?
Yes_____ **No**_____

2 Check which statements seem to be most accurate:
A Christian who feels spiritually dry inside . . .
___ Is committing some kind of really bad sin that makes him or her feel that way
___ Is not doing the right things such as reading the Bible, praying, or going to church
___ Is doing something bad but refusing to face it
___ Can be a solid, committed Christian without any major sin in his or her life
___ Is just imagining everything—recently ate some bad pizza
___ Is working too hard doing good and needs to eat, drink, and be merry

3 Read Psalm 143:4-10. Write several one-word descriptions of how the author of this psalm is feeling:_____

_____

4 What do you think a person who finds themselves feeling spiritually dry should do? Give a grade to each response (**A=Great, F= Fail**):
___ Give up being a Christian
___ Stop going to church or reading the Bible until you feel different
___ Don't say anything to anyone or they might think you are a failure as a Christian
___ Ask for prayer
___ Tell God about it
___ Tell an older or more mature Christian about how you feel
___ Ignore the feeling and continue to do what is right
___ Become depressed
Your idea:_____

5 Which do you think should determine our Christianity?
___ How spiritual or close to God we feel at any given moment
___ The fact that we are really a child of God and that he would not abandon us

6 Why did you choose your answer?

DRY INSIDE

Topic: Feeling spiritually dry.
Biblical Basis: Psalm 143

Purpose of this Session:

Spiritual dryness is experienced by almost every Christian at one time or another. Junior highers are no exception, but many of them have not had the years of experience in the Christian life to know what is going on inside of them. They often panic or take the flatness as a signal that it is time to look elsewhere for spiritual fulfillment.

There aren't always simple reasons for spiritual dryness. Kids will often think that it is the result of some sin in their life. While this can be the case, dry periods often show up in the lives of those who are living exemplary Christian lives.

This TalkSheet is designed to help kids understand that spiritual dryness happens to the best among us, and that the Christian life is not driven by feelings, but rather the fact that Christians are part of God's family.

To Introduce the Topic:

Find out which kid in the room has the most geographically-distant relative. Next, find out who has a relative that they have not heard from in over a year. Ask who in their family writes their relatives. Talk about what it takes to maintain a long-distance relationship. Use some of these ideas to introduce the first discussion question.

The Discussion:

Item #1: Start off by sharing a time in your life when you were spiritually dry. Next, have several willing students talk about the times they have felt God was far off or that spiritual things had little interest to them. Look for any common threads to their experiences.

Item #2: Talk about the fact that dryness can have many different causes, not all of them related to something we have or have not done.

Item #3: Have several willing students share their answers. Discuss the feelings and actions of the psalmist. Point out that the psalmist does not identify any particular reason for feeling so distant from God.

Item #4: Talk about possible solutions for spiritual dryness. Discuss what actions would be wise or unwise to take.

Item #5: Explore the idea that the *fact* of our relationship with God is what determines the reality of our faith, not our emotional state at a given time.

To Close the Session:

Sum up what you have discovered about spiritual dryness, its causes, and the relationship between your faith and your feelings. Ask your students to join you in a responsive reading of Psalm 143.

Outside Activity:

Have your students go on a Scripture Search and put together a collection of verses that assure them of God's presence at all times. (Gideon Bibles can be a great help, as they list a number of such verses in the front pages of their Bibles.) When you have collected the verses from your students, write them on pieces of poster board cut out to look like drops of water and distribute them as bookmarkers.

The Seeds of Smart Living

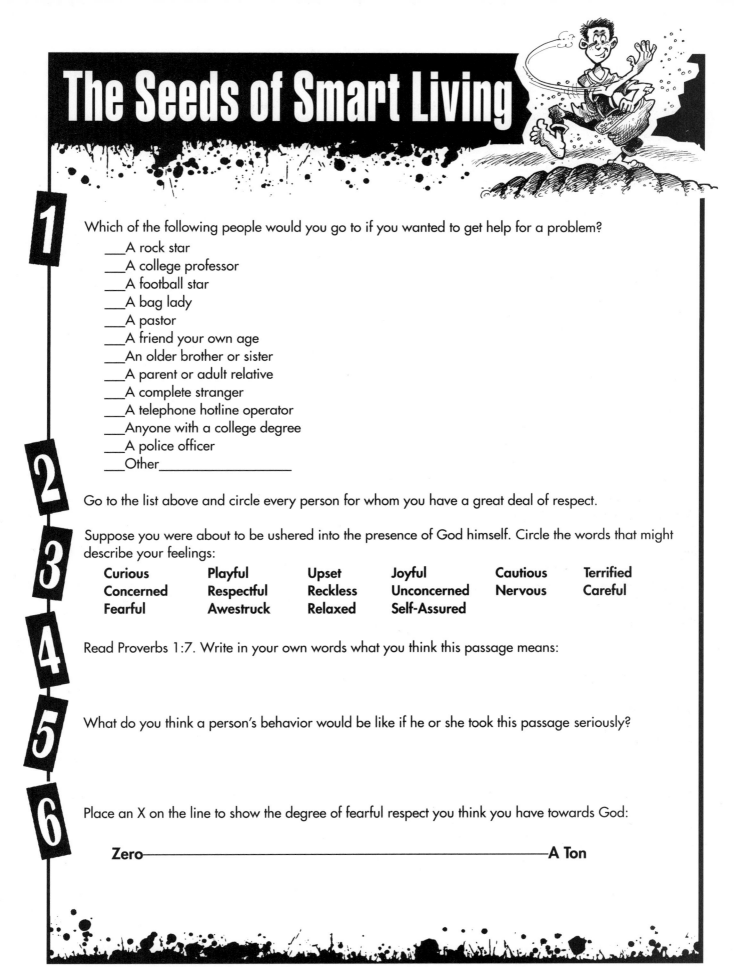

1 Which of the following people would you go to if you wanted to get help for a problem?

___A rock star
___A college professor
___A football star
___A bag lady
___A pastor
___A friend your own age
___An older brother or sister
___A parent or adult relative
___A complete stranger
___A telephone hotline operator
___Anyone with a college degree
___A police officer
___Other_____

2 Go to the list above and circle every person for whom you have a great deal of respect.

3 Suppose you were about to be ushered into the presence of God himself. Circle the words that might describe your feelings:

Curious	**Playful**	**Upset**	**Joyful**	**Cautious**	**Terrified**
Concerned	**Respectful**	**Reckless**	**Unconcerned**	**Nervous**	**Careful**
Fearful	**Awestruck**	**Relaxed**	**Self-Assured**		

4 Read Proverbs 1:7. Write in your own words what you think this passage means:

5 What do you think a person's behavior would be like if he or she took this passage seriously?

6 Place an X on the line to show the degree of fearful respect you think you have towards God:

Zero——————————————————————————**A Ton**

THE SEEDS OF SMART LIVING

Topic: Reverence for God creates wisdom.
Biblical Basis: Proverbs 1

Purpose of the Topic:

This TalkSheet is designed to help students consider the relationship between a respectful and reverential fear of God and making wise choices. Since kids often seek wisdom from many unwise sources, it is vital to establish the rationale and source for godly wisdom. By the end of this session, students will be able to determine their own degree of respect for God.

To Introduce the Topic:

Ask your students to relate a time they received an electrical shock. Discuss how they came to receive the shock, their surprise at the power of regular house current, and most importantly, what they learned in relationship to electricity. Have students talk about their respect for the power of electricity. This is a great way to tie into the concept of God's awesome power, the kind of "fear" or respect we ought to have for his person, and the wisdom that comes from this reverential fear.

The Discussion:

Item #1: Ask your students to select the people they most value and respect for their wisdom. Invite kids to explain their choices. Ask what other names came to mind to fill in the blank.
Item #2: See how many of those that your students checked are one and the same with those they circled. Help your students see how wisdom and respect go hand in hand.
Item #3: Focus on the fact that being in God's presence is not a trivial matter; but for the believer, neither is it a cause for terror. A healthy view of God is one that mixes awe, reverence, and respectful fear (such as how one would approach electricity after a good shock). Many people today have lost the sense of God's tremendous majesty and incredible power. One rarely seeks wisdom from someone he or she doesn't respect.
Item #4: Have several willing students share their paraphrases and comments.
Item #5: Help students see the connection between a healthy, reverential fear of God, and the wise living and choices that will result from that fear.
Item #6: Allow kids to determine privately where they land when it comes to real respect and reverence towards God. Let them know that they will not be asked to share their answers to this question; it's a matter between them and God.

To Close the Session:

God motivates us to serve him by his incredible power, but he never *makes* us revere him. (In the end though, all will revere him.) Not all who claim to revere him actually do. Help your students see that one mark of a person who truly "fears" God will be a genuine desire to be obedient to his will. The path to foolish and destructive living is to not give God the respect and position in our lives that he deserves.

Outside Activities:

Have your students look around this week for other examples of things they respectfully fear. Tell them to consider how those things that they respectfully fear compare to God Almighty. Challenge them to reevaluate what they respect and don't respect in light of God's priorities.

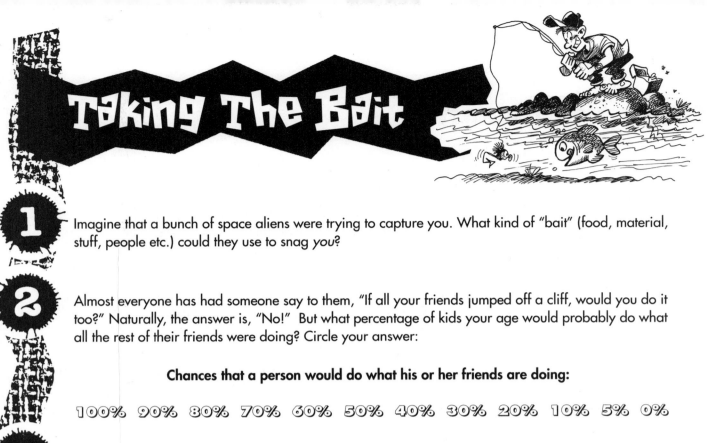

Taking The Bait

1 Imagine that a bunch of space aliens were trying to capture you. What kind of "bait" (food, material, stuff, people etc.) could they use to snag *you*?

2 Almost everyone has had someone say to them, "If all your friends jumped off a cliff, would you do it too?" Naturally, the answer is, "No!" But what percentage of kids your age would probably do what all the rest of their friends were doing? Circle your answer:

Chances that a person would do what his or her friends are doing:

100%   90%   80%   70%   60%   50%   40%   30%   20%   10%   5%   0%

3 Read Proverbs 1:10-19. How might a foolish kid respond to those words? What about a wise kid? Write your answers below:

Foolish Kid	**Wise Kid**
_____	_____
_____	_____

4 This proverb says that the people who do wrong get trapped in their own net. How can people who do wrong things get tangled up in traps of their own creation?

5 Do you agree or disagree with the following statements? (Circle your answers.)

A person with friends who do the wrong thing should change friends.
 AGREE   **DISAGREE**

A person with friends who do the wrong things should try to help them do the right things.
 AGREE   **DISAGREE**

A person who hangs with friends who do the wrong things is likely to do those things too.
 AGREE   **DISAGREE**

TAKING THE BAIT

Topic: The lure of bad friends.
Biblical Basis: Proverbs 1

Purpose of this Session:

Many young teens assume that they are their own person and are influenced little by their friends. Those who observe teens for any length of time have just the opposite opinion. This TalkSheet is designed to help students see that the enticement of bad friends can lead to a life of misery and despair.

To Introduce the Topic:

Bring in several varieties of traps and lures—mousetraps, fishing lures, etc. Discuss how each of them works, what kind of creature it works with, what kind of bait that is used, and the probabilities of the creature escaping from the trap.

   Another fun introductory activity is called "Using Your Noodle." Put dollar bills in the bait slots of several mousetraps. Set the traps. Divide into teams and give each team a few uncooked spaghetti noodles. Instruct your teams to use their noodles to retrieve the dollar, without springing the traps. Use this activity as a way to introduce discussion Item #1.

The Discussion:

Item #1: Most kids know what they are likely to be tempted with. Ask kids to reveal those items. Find out if your students think others are aware of their weak spots.

Item #2: Allow your group to circle their best-guess estimates, then see which kids have varying opinions and the reasons for the variance. Let them defend their opinions to one another.

Item #3: After your students have looked at these passages and commented on the possible responses, ask how many students have heard the very same responses coming from the mouths of their friends. Point out how relevant this passage of Scripture is to the present-day lives of teens.

Item #4: Invite as many kids as possible to share examples of how people they know have tangled themselves up with their own poor choices. See if your kids can guess what their mindsets might have been as they made the choices that snared them.

Item #5: This activity will help your students to see how they can use wisdom to temper the influence of friends. Discuss the difficulties in breaking off with friends who are simply not good influences. Discuss the opportunities and dangers involved in trying to influence those friends for good.

To Close the Session:

Although many of us think we are the exception, the truth is that "bad company corrupts good morals." We must be very careful in who we choose to hang out with, because not all who profess to like us have our best interests in mind. God may use us to influence our friends towards good. In fact, one of the greatest things a young teen can do is to draw his or her friends towards God. But we must be strong in the faith and realize our own limitations and areas of weakness in order not to be pulled into the company of those who we are trying to reach.

Outside Activity:

Challenge your group to create an event that would be attractive to their friends and acquaintances who are heading down a troubled path. A Christian concert or a fun, high-energy "Fifth Quarter" postgame outreach event could introduce their friends to those whose lives and words could influence them towards Christ.

SMARTY-PANTS

1 What shows how smart people are? Mark the following qualities below in their order of importance for showing "smarts," with **#1** being the smartest:

___ Grades they get in school   ___ The ease in which they learn a skill

___ What they do with what they know   ___ How few mistakes they make

___ How respected they are by others   ___ How well they get along with others

___ How well they do their particular job   ___ How high their IQ test scores are

___ Other:_____

2 If *Genius* was 100 points and *Total Moron* was zero, how smart do you think you are for a kid your age? _____ How many points do you think you will have by age 30? _____

3 Have you ever *really* thought you were right about something . . . and it turned out you were wrong? Describe what happened and how you felt:

4 Read Proverbs 3:5-6. Write down the three most important ideas stated in the passage:

_____

_____

_____

5 If you can't trust your own heart and thoughts, who or what can you trust? Circle the best answer(s):

    Your friends   **Your schoolteachers**

    Your pastor   **The Bible**

    The leaders of our country   **Yourself**

6 How does someone acknowledge God in all of his or her ways?

SMARTY-PANTS

Topic: Trusting God rather than yourself.
Biblical Basis: Proverbs 3

Purpose of this Session:

Young teens are in the process of making the break from their parents and becoming their own persons. Part of this process is moving away from trusting their parents' word for everything to thinking on their own. Something has to become the governing authority for the teenager. More often than not, that governing authority is a group of friends, the tug of awakening senses, or the usually immature logic of their own thinking. This TalkSheet will help students to learn that God wants teens and adults alike to abandon all pretension of wisdom and seek his ways. The reward for this sensible thinking is a life that remains on course.

To Introduce the Topic:

Create a Thinking Cap out of an old hat, weird decorations, and glue. Get ahold of some small fun prizes, a timer, and some *Trivial Pursuit* questions for a game of "Brain Head."

Have your group sit in chairs around the room. Set your timer for five minutes. When you read a question, the first person to stand may answer. If the person answers correctly, he or she gets to wear the Thinking Cap. Ask another question; if someone else answers correctly, that person gets the Thinking Cap. Keep this up until the timer rings, then award a prize to whoever is wearing the hat at the time. If time allows, reset the timer and start again.

Use this game as an introduction to the topic of how to be a smart thinker.

The Discussion:

Item #1: Explore what qualities define "smartness" to your students. List the top five they suggest. Note if there is a strong pull towards use of information or sociability, as opposed to academic achievement, as the essence of being smart (this is commonly called "street smart").
Item #2: Having a working definition of what it is to be smart, students can estimate where they are now and where they might be in the area of "smarts."
Item #3: Have several willing students share their experiences. Add an experience of your own. Point out that all of us, no matter how brilliant we think we are, can be absolutely wrong at the very time we think we are right.
Item #4: Make sure the kids have identified the three ideas (trust in God with all your heart; don't rely on your own understanding; acknowledge God in all that you do). Note that the Bible teaches that all the might of human thinking is not to be trusted. God alone is the only one who has the wisdom to guide our lives. Ask kids what they think could result from thinking we can figure out life on our own.
Item #5: Discuss where and how we get God's wisdom and guidance—through his Word, prayer, and the counsel of family, trusted Christian ministers, and caring friends.
Item #6: Discuss what it means to acknowledge God in all areas of our lives. Encourage the kids to come up with specific ways that they can do this. Talk about *how* what we say and do sends a message to others about God.

To Close the Session:

Summarize that no amount of human genius or understanding is safe enough to use as a map for getting through this world. God's ideas, values, and directions are what it takes to walk a straight road. His words are found in the Bible and through prayer.

A person who is truly smart will realize that God is smarter still, and will try to discover what he has to say about various choices facing us in life. A truly smart person will follow what God says, even if it doesn't seem to make sense at the time.

Outside Activity:

Collect taped interviews from people who have learned the hard way that God's way of thinking makes way more sense than leaning on their own understanding. Play it to your kids to show the brilliance of a young person who learns this lesson early rather than by the folly of a painful experience.

DO-GOODER

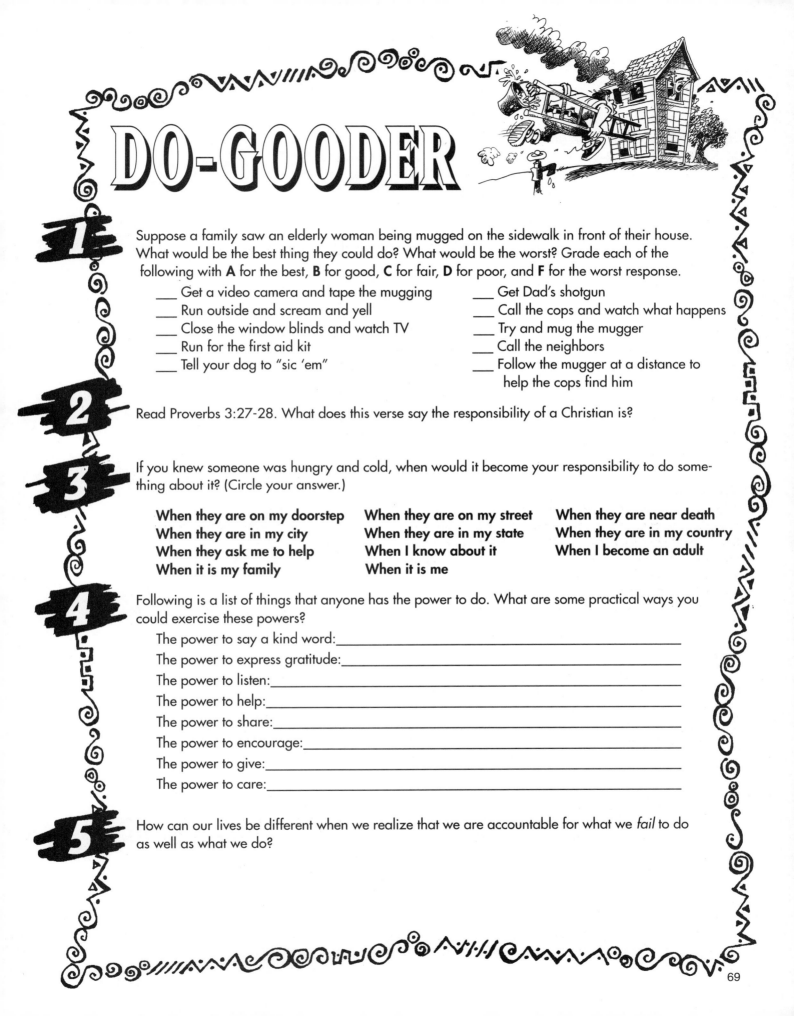

1 Suppose a family saw an elderly woman being mugged on the sidewalk in front of their house. What would be the best thing they could do? What would be the worst? Grade each of the following with **A** for the best, **B** for good, **C** for fair, **D** for poor, and **F** for the worst response.

___ Get a video camera and tape the mugging
___ Run outside and scream and yell
___ Close the window blinds and watch TV
___ Run for the first aid kit
___ Tell your dog to "sic 'em"

___ Get Dad's shotgun
___ Call the cops and watch what happens
___ Try and mug the mugger
___ Call the neighbors
___ Follow the mugger at a distance to help the cops find him

2 Read Proverbs 3:27-28. What does this verse say the responsibility of a Christian is?

3 If you knew someone was hungry and cold, when would it become your responsibility to do something about it? (Circle your answer.)

When they are on my doorstep   **When they are on my street**   **When they are near death**
When they are in my city   **When they are in my state**   **When they are in my country**
When they ask me to help   **When I know about it**   **When I become an adult**
When it is my family   **When it is me**

4 Following is a list of things that anyone has the power to do. What are some practical ways you could exercise these powers?

The power to say a kind word:_____

The power to express gratitude:_____

The power to listen:_____

The power to help:_____

The power to share:_____

The power to encourage:_____

The power to give:_____

The power to care:_____

5 How can our lives be different when we realize that we are accountable for what we *fail* to do as well as what we do?

DO-GOODER

Topic: Using our power to do good.
Biblical Basis: Proverbs 3

Purpose of this Session:

Christian young people often are bombarded with actions or activities that are to be avoided. Less frequently are they encouraged to engage in actions and activities that do good to those they have the power to help. It is these acts which spell out the reality of faith to others. This TalkSheet encourages your kids to explore options that can stretch their faith in practical ways.

To Introduce the Topic:

Tell your kids that they are to imagine that they have become the president of the United States for one day. They have the power to do all kinds of things. Have your students share what they would do if they had that kind of power at their fingertips. Some kids may suggest ideas that are silly or self-serving, others may come up with ideas that are very positive. The point is, all of the kids would use the power available to them for something. Let your group know that they will be discussing how they can use the power they have right now.

The Discussion:

Item #1: Ask your young people to share their grades for the various behaviors. Ask why they gave a failing grade to the ones they did. Note any patterns to their responses.

Item #2: Have your kids discuss their answers. The point you want them to grasp is that to do good when we have an opportunity is the *duty* of every Christian.

Item #3: Help your young people see that the our obligation to help those in need extends universally. Brainstorm ways that a young person could help someone who was hungry and cold in a faraway land. Guide them to specfic ideas, such as sponsoring a child through Compassion International or World Vision, supporting church missionaries who are working in poor countries, etc.

Item #4: Help the kids to brainstorm practical ways that they might do good with the power that they have. Have willing students share their answers, and help kids to build upon one another's answers.

Item #5: Help kids identify what changes *they* could make to enable them to do all the good that is within their power.

To Close the Session:

Challenge the students to consider putting their faith into action in small but powerful ways. While we may not have people starving for food near us, we often know kids who are starving for acceptance and kindness. We can express thanks and gratitude to parents, teachers, and friends. We can find ways to serve in simple ways, by washing the church van or by helping a brother or sister with chores. We can write a letter or make a phone call that will brighten a grandparent's day. Help students discover what practical things they *can* do right now.

Outside Activity:

Invite your students to set aside a special day, as a group, to be "do-gooders." You could start by cleaning a portion of the church, preparing and delivering a meal for a shut-in, and other viable projects. Once kids experience the satisfaction that comes from this kind of service, they'll be raring for more.

Lazybones

1 How would you define laziness?

2 Match the consequences of laziness with their source:

Late to work	Flunk school
Watch too much TV	Make a strange noise at the band concert
Don't get around to doing homework	Miss out on much of the day
Neglect to write thank-you cards	Rush to get the chores done at the last minute
Don't bother to practice instrument	Grandma doesn't send you anything
Sleep in late	Get a brain full of mush
Put off doing chores	Get fired

3 Read Proverbs 6:6-11. What does this passage say will happen to the lazy person? What example is given of the industrious person? What qualities does the ant display?

_____

_____

_____

4 Would you bail the lazy man out of his trouble? Why or why not?

5 Which statement is most true for you:

___ I feel much better about myself and my life when I have been productive and worked hard.
___ I feel much better about myself and my life when I lay around and do nothing.

6 What is the right amount of hours in a day for a person to be involved in the following activities? Keep in mind there are only twenty-four hours in a day. Check the ones you think are wasteful if done too much.

___Sleeping	___Sports or play	___Watching TV
___Reading	___Talking on the phone	___Thinking
___Listening to music	___Hanging out with friends	___School or studies
___Devotions	___Talking to parents	___Eating
___Doing chores or going to work	___Other	

7 What areas to you tend to be lazy in? What could you do to make your life more fun and productive?

LAZYBONES

Topic: Being productive.
Biblical Basis: Proverbs 6

Purpose of this Session:
Everyone has twenty-four hours in a day, yet some people seem to get a whole lot done with those hours, while others barely get off the couch. One of the biblical principles to security and godliness is that of wise productivity. Young people are beginning the practices that will become habits of a lifetime. This TalkSheet is designed to help students learn to discipline and control their time so that they can not only work well, but rest well. They can have a life that is productive and becomes a contribution by following God's principles.

To Introduce the Topic:
Have your kids stand in the middle of the room. On a chalkboard or overhead, write the statement: "I could get all A's in school." Ask the kids to go to one end of the room if they agree with the statement, and the other end of the room if they disagree. Next, add to the statement by saying things like, "I could get all A's in school if I was given $50 for each A I brought home." See how many kids move to the agree side. Keep upping the money amount until all of the kids agree with your statement, or until you are offering $100,000 for each A. Point out that if the motivation is high enough, almost everyone will work hard to get straight A's. The thing that keeps many of us from doing what we are capable of is our own laziness.

The Discussion:
Item #1: Have your students share their definitions of laziness. Ask, "How would you rate yourselves? Productive or lazy?"
Item #2: Discuss the results of a lazy lifestyle. Talk about how habits that start when we are young can lead to more disastrous results when we get older. Share an example of laziness in your own life, and the consequences you faced because of it.
Item #3: Point out that an ant does not wait to be told what to do, but takes the initiative to accomplish what needs to be done.
Item #4: Discuss the situation of the lazy man. Should he be bailed out of trouble? Why or why not? Allow for debate; don't try to force the whole group to a consensus.
Item #5: Ask kids, "Why is it true for most people that they feel better about themselves and their lives when they work hard?" Help kids to see that industry does have its own reward—the satisfaction that leads to a positive and healthy self-image.
Item #6: Allow your students to explore realistic amounts of time for work, play, and rest. Point out that the time they have allowed may change as they grow older and assume more responsibilities.
Item #7: Here is an opportunity for you to challenge your kids to break some slothful habits and to rearrange some areas of their lives. Encourage them to discuss what practical things they can think of to help with this process.

To Close the Session:
Encourage your students to be wise stewards of their time and energy. Explain to them that they only have one lifetime to live and that they can use it to its fullest, or squander it. Point out that while watching TV and playing video games may be fun, they are also great devourers of time with little practical return. Challenge them to pay their dues in hard work for anything—from playing the guitar to getting good grades—rather than thinking they will magically get the rewards for those things in the future.

Outside Activity:
Solicit volunteers who will commit to give up TV and video games for one week. At your next meeting, see how many were able to achieve the goal and how they used their time. Ask them if their experience will make a difference in how they will approach TV viewing and video-game playing in the future.

I'D BE LYING IF I SAID I WAS HONEST

 1 Would you go to a doctor that you knew cheated his or her way through medical school?

Why or why not?

2 Circle any of the following that you would consider to be dishonest:

Telling a caller that your mom isn't home when she just doesn't want to come to the phone
Agreeing that a friend's dress is nice when you really think it is ugly
Keeping the extra money that you have accidentally been given in change for a purchase
Taking fruit off a neighbor's tree (who merely lets it rot) without asking
Passing on something that is supposed to be a secret
Taking the blame for something you didn't do in order to help another person save face
Taking the credit for a report you copied from another source
Saying you are going to the mall when you plan to meet someone there and then leave

3 When you are dishonest, what do you worry about most?

 **4** Read Proverbs 10:9. Do you agree ___ or disagree___ with the statement?
Why?

Explain in your own words what you think the writer means:

 5 Circle **OFTEN**, **SOMETIMES**, or **NEVER** for each of the following:

a. I cheat in school or sports	**OFTEN**	**SOMETIMES**	**NEVER**
b. I stretch the truth	**OFTEN**	**SOMETIMES**	**NEVER**
c. I trick or deceive my parents	**OFTEN**	**SOMETIMES**	**NEVER**
d. I keep my word and promises	**OFTEN**	**SOMETIMES**	**NEVER**
e. I take what is not mine to take	**OFTEN**	**SOMETIMES**	**NEVER**

 **6** Draw connecting lines between the Scripture verses and the appropriate statements:

Psalm 37:21	A truthful person does not deceive
Exodus 23:1	Do not steal
Ephesians 4:25	If you borrow, be sure to repay
Leviticus 19:11	Speak truthfully to each other
Proverbs 14:5	Don't spread false stories

I'D BE LYING IF I SAID I WAS HONEST

Topic: Integrity.
Biblical Basis: Proverbs 10

Purpose of this Session:

The battle to live a life of integrity never ends. For many teens, the idea of a life of integrity is a foreign concept. Many in our culture push the ethics of expedience, and integrity is often anything but expedient.

Young teens face challenges to integrity constantly. Will they be true to their word? Will they cheat at sports, games, or schoolwork? Will they deceive others to get out of trouble? Will they embellish events to increase their social stature? Naturally, God sets high standards for integrity—but as high as they are, they are achievable and rewarding, especially when living with integrity becomes a habit.

To Introduce the Topic:

A few days before this session, send out a mailing to your students reminding them of the upcoming meeting and promising a prize for each one who brings the mailer with them. A good number will show up with mailer in hand. Pretend that you forgot about your promise, or that you changed your mind when it comes time for the kids to collect their prize. Then start your session by asking how many students were surprised and disappointed that you did not keep your word. Ask them if they feel they could trust you in the future. Finally, introduce your topic—then tell your students that you *do* have prizes for those who brought mailers which you will give out at the end of the session.

The Discussion:

Item #1: Let your kids point out the obvious—why they wouldn't trust a doctor who cheated through medical school. Throw in a few more examples, such as: A president who lied to get into office, an athlete who set a world record while using illegal drugs, or a police officer who took bribes from rich crooks. Point out that honesty is one of the pillars of society because trust between people is essential.

Item #2: Allow your group to explain why some of the actions listed are dishonest or not. Be prepared to discuss what could be said that would be gentle, but still honest, in some of these situations. Allow for some disagreement here—every situation noted doesn't necessarily have a black-and-white answer.

Item #3: Discuss the downside of dishonesty. Most liars, cheaters, promise breakers, and thieves live in fear that they will be caught or discovered. Fear and guilt are not fun feelings.

Item #4: Talk about the value of a mind and heart at peace. Discuss the safety in being honest.

Item #5: Without asking kids to be too revealing, see how many will concede that they struggle with honesty. See if you can detect any common areas of struggle. To help your students understand that they're not alone, share an appropriate example of an area where you struggle with maintaining integrity.

Item #6: When your kids have completed these, say, "God lays out standards for integrity. He is willing to forgive all shortcomings, but he wants honesty to become the habit of our lives."

To Close the Session:

Most kids are aware that honesty is the best policy, even when it is painful. Give your students a chance to affirm their commitment to being people of integrity by creating a *Pledge of Integrity* document which your kids can sign if they are willing to maintain a life of honesty. And make sure to give out the prizes that you promised at the beginning of the session!

Outside Activity:

Ask your students to attempt to keep their word for the upcoming week. They are not to make any promises, even small ones, unless they are willing to keep them. Assign partners who will check up on one another and encourage one another to stay on course.

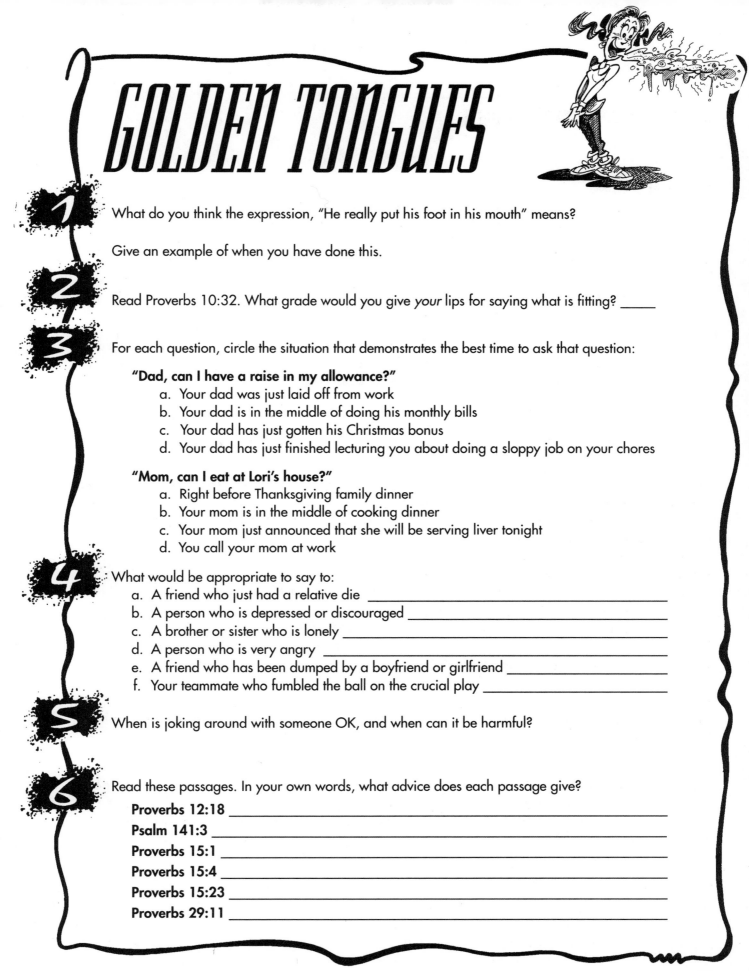

GOLDEN TONGUES

1 What do you think the expression, "He really put his foot in his mouth" means?

Give an example of when you have done this.

2 Read Proverbs 10:32. What grade would you give *your* lips for saying what is fitting? _____

3 For each question, circle the situation that demonstrates the best time to ask that question:

"Dad, can I have a raise in my allowance?"
    a. Your dad was just laid off from work
    b. Your dad is in the middle of doing his monthly bills
    c. Your dad has just gotten his Christmas bonus
    d. Your dad has just finished lecturing you about doing a sloppy job on your chores

"Mom, can I eat at Lori's house?"
    a. Right before Thanksgiving family dinner
    b. Your mom is in the middle of cooking dinner
    c. Your mom just announced that she will be serving liver tonight
    d. You call your mom at work

4 What would be appropriate to say to:
    a. A friend who just had a relative die _____
    b. A person who is depressed or discouraged _____
    c. A brother or sister who is lonely _____
    d. A person who is very angry _____
    e. A friend who has been dumped by a boyfriend or girlfriend _____
    f. Your teammate who fumbled the ball on the crucial play _____

5 When is joking around with someone OK, and when can it be harmful?

6 Read these passages. In your own words, what advice does each passage give?
    Proverbs 12:18 _____
    Psalm 141:3 _____
    Proverbs 15:1 _____
    Proverbs 15:4 _____
    Proverbs 15:23 _____
    Proverbs 29:11 _____

GOLDEN TONGUES

Topic: Controlling our speech.
Biblical Basis: Proverbs 10

Purpose of this Session:

Young people often use words to wound and hurt one another. Sometimes the wounds are accidental; other times, they are aimed and intentional. It is common for young teens to say the wrong thing at the wrong time. This TalkSheet is designed to help your students explore what to say, how to say it, and when to say nothing at all.

To Introduce the Topic:

Bring paper, markers, glue sticks, and a number of photos you've cut out from magazines and newspapers. Hand the materials out to your kids. Ask them to select one photo and come up with a dumb phrase to paste as a "word balloon" on the photo. When everyone has finished, share the results and enjoy some laughs. Move on to the lesson by telling your students that while what they have done today may be fiction, we often say things just as dumb in real life. Tell them that they will be discussing the idea of using speech that fits the occasion.

The Discussion:

Item #1: Discuss what it means to say the wrong thing at the wrong time. Share an incident when you put your foot in your mouth, then have a few willing students share their stories.

Item #2: Have kids share their grades. Share your grade, then say, "If we could be graded on what we said, many of us would have a pretty low grade average."

Item #3: Use these questions to discuss timing. Say something like, "Some things can be right to say, but at the wrong time. We need to be aware of *when* to speak as well as *what* to say."

Item #4: Have your kids brainstorm what would be apt responses to people in the situations listed. List the best responses, and the right time to say them, on a chalkboard. Ask your students if they have had any of these events happen to them. If any volunteer an answer, have them share how they felt and what would have been the right thing for someone to say to them.

Item #5: Many young people joke around and make fun of each other. Often this is just good-natured jesting. Sometimes though, young teens can become very cruel, even ganging up on some poor individual to rip them to shreds. Have kids share their views on the limits to joking, when it can backfire, and when it can become hurtful.

Item #6: Have a few willing kids share their answers. Help them to understand the principles behind appropriate speech: **1.** Being kind and gentle with our words; **2.** Knowing *when* to say something; **3.** Keeping our angry and harsh words under control.

To Close the Session:

Summarize the points that have been made during the TalkSheet discussion. Say something like, "We can all get along much better with other people when we have the wisdom to know what to say, when to say it, and when not to say anything." If time allows, select a few volunteers to roleplay the situations described in Item #4. After each roleplay, let the group evaluate how the characters did in speaking appropriately. Point out that God wants us to use our words to build up others rather than tear them down.

Outside Activity:

Ask your students to think of one person who they have not always responded to in the best manner. It could be a parent whom they treat disrespectfully, or a kid in school who is the butt of all their jokes. Challenge your students to make a list of ten uplifting things that they will try to say to that person in the upcoming week. Check with your kids the next week to see how things went.

A RING IN A PIG'S SNOUT

1 A person is made up of two intertwined things: The package on the outside and the contents on the inside. Put a **P** (for package) on any of the items listed below that deal primarily with the outside of a person and a **C** (for contents) that deals with what a person is like on the inside. (Some items may have both a **P** and a **C**.)

____Strength	____Courage	____Faith	____Beauty	____Kindness
____Friendliness	____Patience	____Self-Control	____Muscles	____Godliness
____Attractiveness	____Ugliness	____Honesty	____Agility	____Imagination
____Humor				

2 What do you think the average person is most concerned about:

____Their package   ____The contents of their package

Why?

3 Read Proverbs 11:22. Which of the following do you think best describes the symbolism used in the passage?

___ Pretty women make better wives than pigs.
___ A beautiful person who is impure and foolish on the inside is a sad waste.
___ Don't waste gold on a dirty pig when you can use it as a wedding ring.
___ A woman with no discretion will hang around with pigs.
___ Pigs and people with no sound judgment are the same.
___ Beautiful people should have wise judgment and pigs should not wear jewelry.

4 True or False?

Most people put more work into how they look than into who they are.	___ T	___ F
A beautiful person can also be ugly.	___ T	___ F
A person who is handsome or pretty will get further in life than someone who is plain looking.	___ T	___ F
A person who is attractive on the outside will probably be attractive on the inside as well.	___ T	___ F

5 Read the following passages. In your own words, write down the qualities these passages describe as important for true beauty:

Galatians 5:22-23 _____

Ephesians 4:22-24 _____

Matthew 5:8 _____

A RING IN A PIG'S SNOUT

Topic: Inner beauty.
Biblical Basis: Proverbs 11

Purpose of this Session:

Young teens are bombarded by a world of attractive and desirable images. They know that appearance is important, and spend much of their time primping and worrying about how they look. What is often lost is the need to put at least an equal amount of time and effort into developing an attractive inner character.

It is a person who is attractive on the outside but who has never developed the ability to make wise choices that the writer of Proverbs equates with a pig (unclean to the Jews) with a gold ring in its nose. This TalkSheet offers an opportunity to talk with your students about working on their character, their spiritual lives, and their personalities with the same fervor that they work on their outside appearance.

To Introduce the Topic:

Locate some books and magazines (e.g., *National Geographic*) that have pictures of "attractive people" from different cultures and eras. Pass the pictures around to your kids, and note that in different times or cultures, the idea of "beauty" can vary widely. Renaissance painters show the beautiful women of their day as quite heavy by our standards; in ancient Hawaiian culture, a 300-pound man was considered very attractive. Tell your students that the discussion today will revolve around beauty, both inner and outer.

The Discussion:

Item #1: Allow your students to explore which of the attributes are external or internal in nature. Allow for debate and disagreement. Discuss which can be both, such as Strength, Attractiveness, Beauty, and Ugliness.
Item #2: Have a few willing students share their answers. If kids are honest, most will admit that the average person worries more about their package. Talk about what creates that focus—the images that are held up to us through the media, and the fragility of our own self-images.
Item #3: Have your kids share their answers. Make sure they've identified the correct answers (numbers two and five). Point out that a pig was considered an unclean animal to the Hebrew writers who authored these proverbs.
Item #4: Use this quiz to stimulate discussion about people who look attractive but whose thinking is mixed up, and those who may not be "beautiful" on the outside, but who have inner qualities and gifts that can take them a long way in life.
Item #5: Help your kids to describe these biblical qualities for inner beauty in their own words. Ask, "How can these qualities be seen in people today?" Invite them to affirm such qualities that they see in one another. Point out how these can get better with age, as distinct from physical beauty.

To Close the Session:

Explain that while it is important to take care of our physical appearance, it is even more important to work on developing our character, spiritual life, and personality. Say, "It is possible to be an attractive fool. The body we have will be shed, but *who* we are will last forever. That's why God wants us to invest in our inner qualities." Encourage your kids to spend time in personal devotions as one way to develop inner beauty.

Outside Activity:

Invite your students to decorate their mirrors at home with Post-It note reminders to put equal work into their souls as they are into their bodies.

TAKER OR GIVER?

1 Circle the last person you bought a gift for with your own money:

Mom	Dad	Brother	Sister	Neighbor	Friend	No one
Teacher	Minister	Aunt	Uncle	Grandma	Grandpa	Self

2 Complete these statements with the words that seem best to you:

A generous person is likely to _____

There is giving and there is receiving. If I had a choice, I would _____

The best way to give a gift is _____

3 What is one gift that you would like to give if you could afford it?

_____

Who would you give it to? _____

Why? _____

4 Check the three best ways to be a giver:

___ **Do someone a favor**   ___ **Lend a hand**

___ **Buy something for someone**   ___ **Put money in the church offering**

___ **Send money to a Third World country**   ___ **Spend time with a lonely senior citizen**

___ **Say something kind to someone**   ___ **Other:_____**

5 Read Proverbs 11:24. What doesn't appear to make sense in this verse? What could the answer be?

6 Match these passages with what they have to say about being a giver:

2 Corinthians 9:7	The person who is generous will be blessed by God
Matthew 6:1-4	We should give with a cheerful attitude
Acts 20:35	We should give quietly and secretly
Proverbs 22:9	Giving really *is* better than receiving

TAKER OR GIVER?

Topic: Developing a generous spirit.
Biblical Basis: Proverbs 11

Purpose of this Session:

Young teens totter on the edge of being childish takers and maturing, generous givers. They are just now starting to make their own money; only recently have some of them actually bought birthday or Christmas gifts from their own earnings. During this stage in life, young people can develop an attitude toward giving that will affect them the rest of their lives.

"Giving" does not mean money alone. It includes actions and time. Young people can learn to give generously even when they are flat broke.

To Introduce the Topic:

Describe the following situation to your students:

"Mrs. Wyman, the elderly widow who lives down the block, will not be home this Halloween evening. She loves the neighborhood children and does not want to disappoint any of them who may come to her house to trick or treat. Mrs. Wyman buys a few bags of candy and pours them in a box outside her house. Above the box she places a sign that says, *Please take ONE.*"

Ask your students to vote thumbs up or thumbs down on the following questions: Will kids respect the sign? *Should* kids respect the wishes of Mrs. Wyman? What would you do if you came upon this situation while you were trick-or-treating? Is Mrs. Wyman expecting too much of human nature? Use this example as a starting point to talk about being a taker or a giver.

The Discussion:

Item #1: Have willing students share their answers. Many may never have bought a gift for someone else; often, they have bought something for themselves. Discuss the reasons and occasions for gift-giving.

Item #2: Explore various ideas your kids have about giving. Some may feel that to be generous is to be taken advantage of; others may feel that getting is more fun than giving. Discuss the benefits in both giving and receiving.

Item #3: Invite your students to discuss who they would give the gift of their dreams to and why. Ask how it would make them feel to be able to give such a gift.

Item #4: Help your kids explore the idea that being a giving person involves more than material gifts. A giver gives in all areas of life, many of which are worth much more than a tangible item.

Item #5: Discuss God's strange, but functional economy: To give is to gain, to die is to live, to be last is to be first. Ask your kids to brainstorm how these principles might apply in modern, real-life situations.

Item #6: Ask the kids to sum up what it means to live a life of godly generosity. Then say, "How can we apply these attributes in our own lives?" Encourage them to give specific examples.

To Close the Session:

Discuss the blessings and benefits that come to both the giver and receiver from a person who has learned to be a giver. Challenge your kids to follow up on the ideas they brainstormed in Item #6.

Outside Activity:

Have each student select the name of one person who they will make a point to be more giving towards the next week. Have them write down a journal of the "gifts" they give to that person, what resulted from their actions, and how the experiences made them feel. Have your kids bring their journals to the next meeting and share what happened.

SINCERELY WRONG

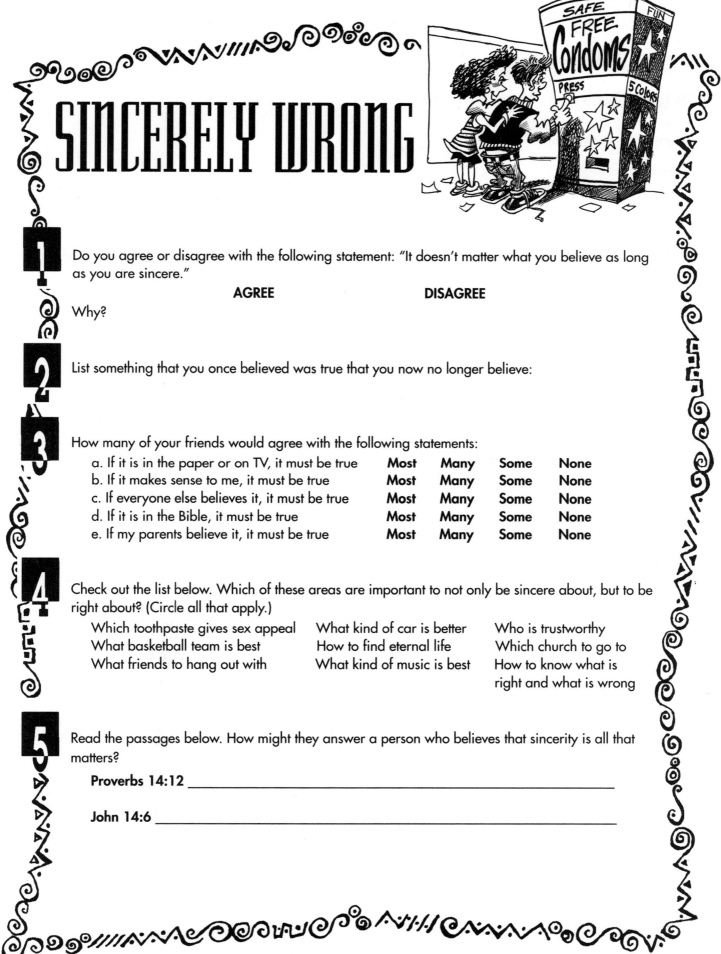

1 Do you agree or disagree with the following statement: "It doesn't matter what you believe as long as you are sincere."

                                AGREE   **DISAGREE**

Why?

2 List something that you once believed was true that you now no longer believe:

3 How many of your friends would agree with the following statements:

a. If it is in the paper or on TV, it must be true	**Most**	**Many**	**Some**	**None**
b. If it makes sense to me, it must be true	**Most**	**Many**	**Some**	**None**
c. If everyone else believes it, it must be true	**Most**	**Many**	**Some**	**None**
d. If it is in the Bible, it must be true	**Most**	**Many**	**Some**	**None**
e. If my parents believe it, it must be true	**Most**	**Many**	**Some**	**None**

4 Check out the list below. Which of these areas are important to not only be sincere about, but to be right about? (Circle all that apply.)

Which toothpaste gives sex appeal	What kind of car is better	Who is trustworthy
What basketball team is best	How to find eternal life	Which church to go to
What friends to hang out with	What kind of music is best	How to know what is right and what is wrong

5 Read the passages below. How might they answer a person who believes that sincerity is all that matters?

    Proverbs 14:12 _____

    John 14:6 _____

SINCERELY WRONG

Topic: God's way is the only way.
Biblical Basis: Proverbs 14

Purpose of this Session:

Most young people, including many within the church, would quickly affirm that it doesn't matter what people believe as long as they sincerely believe it. This faulty line of thinking flies in the face of Christ's words proclaiming himself to be the only source of life-giving truth (see John 14:6). This perspective can also foster a mood of false tolerance. Racism is not acceptable simply because some sincerely believe in it.

Kids need to know that truth is more than mere sincerity. This TalkSheet helps them probe into the blurred thinking of the world and compare it with the crystalline teaching of the Bible.

To Introduce the Topic:

Ask your students, "Do any of you know why Native Americans were called Indians by the early European explorers?" (Allow a few kids to suggest answers.) "The reason is because Columbus thought that he had landed in India. He did not know that he had discovered a new continent.

"Columbus sincerely believed that these dark-skinned people were from India. But his sincerity didn't change the fact that he was wrong, and his error is why Native Americans are mistakenly referred to as 'Indians' to this day."

The Discussion:

Item #1: Let the students discover where they stand on the issue of sincerity being the basis for truth. Invite them to discuss why they agree or disagree. Don't try to generate a consensus at this point.
Item #2: Have kids share some things they used to believe in (such as Santa Claus, the moon is full of green cheese, there are monsters under the bed, etc.). Ask, "What changed those beliefs? What do you think about those who continue to believe in things you would regard as folk tales or superstitions?"
Item #3: Discuss what sources we tend to believe. Ask kids why they regard those sources as credible. Challenge kids to think about the trustworthiness of the sources of information they rely on.
Item #4: Have a few volunteers share their answers. Help your kids to discern between things that are not that crucial, and things that are vital to get right. Ask, "What do you think could happen to people who think they are smart enough to make their own way in life?"
Item #5: Discuss the implications of these passages. What options do they give to people who feel that whatever they sincerely believe is legitimate?

To Close the Session:

Summarize the concept of ultimate truth found in God's Word. Say something like, "While sincerity is a noble feeling, it does not keep us from being sincerely wrong. The teachings of Scripture are our source for truth. They are solid, even if people find them uncomfortable." Challenge your students to think carefully about the various "truths" that they hear and to compare them with the Word of God.

Outside Activity:

Help your students create a Nonsense Meter. Make it out of junk electric parts and a cowbell. Pull it out and ring it as a fun gimmick whenever some wild story, stupid idea, or tall tale is being discussed in your group.

cheer up!

1 Circle which two things would brighten you up the most if you were depressed:

A funny movie	Hearing a favorite song	Singing out loud
Goofing off with friends	A giant ice cream sundae	Other:_____
A phone call from a friend	A good joke	

2 Agree or disagree: "Cheerfulness is contagious."

_____ **AGREE**   _____ **DISAGREE**

Why?

3 True or False:

___ Having a cheerful disposition is something you are born with.
___ Cheerful people don't have any problems.
___ Cheerfulness and being a clown are the same thing.
___ A person who is cheerful is likely to have more friends than someone who is not.
___ A person can learn to be more cheerful.
___ An unpleasant task is made more tolerable by a cheerful outlook.

4 Read Proverbs 15:30, 17:22, and Psalm 32:11. When you have read them, pretend you are a doctor. Write out a "prescription" for your patient (Ima Sourpuss) based on what you have discovered.

Patient's Name: *ImaSourpuss*

Prescribing Physician: *Lord N. Heaven*

Treatment recommended:

Probable results:

Rx

5 Select one of the scenarios below. How could you react cheerfully when facing that situation?

a. Your plans with your friends are squashed because some long-lost relatives have just arrived in town.
b. The guy you secretly liked now has a girlfriend.
c. Your team lost the big playoff game.
d. Your older sister is in a particularly nasty mood.
e. You have been grounded for longer than you think appropriate for your "crime."
f. A friend borrowed your favorite jacket and returned it with a huge stain.

CHEER UP!

Topic: Developing a cheerful attitude.
Biblical Basis: Proverbs 15, 17

Purpose of this Session:

Young people are learning that there are attitudes that can help them and attitudes that can hinder them. One of the most helpful attitudes they can develop is cheerfulness. People with an upbeat, cheerful outlook tend to be well-liked. Since teens often struggle with feeling unliked, this comes as good news.

Cheerfulness will ease the conflict points that are natural in the life of a teenager. It will improve relationships with parents, family, and friends, and reduce some of the trauma of the developing years.

This TalkSheet will help your kids see that a cheerful attitude, even about difficult situations, can make all the difference in the world.

To Introduce the Topic:

Start off by asking for kids to share funny scenes they've seen in recent movies or some funny (*clean*) jokes. Have a few stories and jokes prepared to throw in yourself. Note how the atmosphere of the meeting changes when humor and cheerfulness is injected.

The Discussion:

Item #1: Have your kids share their answers. Encourage them to add their own examples. Discuss what tends to cheer us up when we are depressed. Ask, "Why do these things brighten us up?"

Item #2: See if your students agree that cheerfulness is contagious. Have them explain their answers. Ask, "Is cheerfulness being contagious a good thing? What makes cheerfulness contagious?" Encourage them to share a few stories where one person got others in a laughing mood.

Item #3: Discuss the nature of cheerfulness and cheerful people. Here is a great opportunity to discuss what makes people cheerful, and what the results of a cheerful attitude can be.

Item #4: Have your kids share their prescriptions. Talk about the medicinal effects of humor on a sad heart. Point out where the real joy and contentment comes from (rejoicing in *the Lord*, Psalm 32:11).

Item #5: Have a few willing students share their responses. Lead a brainstorming session with the whole group, encouraging kids to help one another to develop solutions to these scenarios. Ask, "What are some practical ways that we can show a positive and cheerful attitude in these situations? What are the results that come from such an attitude?"

To Close the Session:

Wrap up the session by talking about the benefits, both for ourselves and others, of developing a cheerful attitude, and trusting God to work out things that are beyond our control. Point out that this does not mean going through life with our heads in the sand, but rather taking an authentically hopeful outlook on life, knowing that everything is in the control of a loving God.

Outside Activity:

Have your kids offer names for a list of people they consider to be cheerful. During the week, interview some of them on an audio or videotape and have them share their secrets to maintaining a cheerful attitude. Share the interviews at your next meeting.

BIG SHOT?

1 When you meet people who think they are better, smarter, or cooler than anyone else, how does it make you feel? (Check all of the descriptions that apply.)

___ I want to bow down at their feet.
___ I want to throw up.
___ I admire how self-assured they are.
___ I want to get as far away from them as I possibly can.
___ I want to be their groupie.
___ I immediately think they must be joking.
___ I figure they must be real insecure on the inside.
___ I feel like they love themselves too much.
___ I want to pop their bubble of self-importance.
___ I want to know the secret of their success.

2 Do you agree or disagree with the following statement: "A person who ignores God is giving the message that they think they know better how to live than God does."

_____ **AGREE**   _____ **DISAGREE**

Why?

3 Read the following verses: Proverbs 16:5; 18-19; 27:2; 29:23; 30:12-13.

What do you get when you have pride in your life?

4 Which of the following would you say are prideful, and which would you say are not? (Put a **Y** for yes, this is pride and an **N** for no, this is not pride.)

___Marge is excited and happy because she won the skating contest.
___Ralph likes to show off all the new stuff he gets.
___Whenever a girl walks by, Miguel starts acting tough and putting down his friends.
___Ignoring the advice from his parents and pastor, Ivan continues to ditch school.
___Gena puts her straight-A report card on the refrigerator door.
___Steve laughs at anyone who can't snowboard as well as he can.
___The English teacher says that God is an invention of those who can't cope with life.
___The guys at the lunch table won't let anyone sit with them unless they're invited.

5 How would a person know that they have the disease of pride? _____

What would the symptoms be?_____

How could the disease of pride be cured? _____

BIG SHOT?

Topic: Destructive pride.
Biblical Basis: Proverbs 16; 27; 29; 30

Purpose of this Session:

All young people are tainted by the disease of pride. Many think of pride as bragging or self-glorification, which it can be. But pride is also found hidden in attitudes that want to make fun of others, or in feelings that "no one can tell *me* what to do." Pride is at its most destructive ebb when it challenges God. Many young people challenge God passively. They simply ignore his commands, even while professing to believe them.

The cure to pride is humility—the realization that we are not any more special than anyone else and that we all melt before God. This TalkSheet will help your students to define pride, to understand its destructive power in their lives, and to explore its cure.

To Introduce the Topic:

Have all your students stand in the center of the room. Tell them to move to the left side of the room if they have ever said to someone else, "My dad can beat up your dad." Have them move to the right side of the room if they have ever said, "My dog (or thing) is better than your dog (or thing)" to another kid. Have them sit down if they were right. Have them stand if they were bluffing or didn't know.

Have your kids offer suggestions as to why people say stuff like this. Use this as a means to begin discussing pride and how humans display it.

The Discussion:

Item #1: Talk about how it feels when confronted with someone who is very prideful. Ask if your kids think that the person is even aware of his or her pride. Explain the difference between people who boast because they are, insecure as opposed to people who boast because they think they are superior.

Item #2: Have a few willing students share their answers. Help your students to define pride. Talk about subtle forms of pride such as resistance, stubbornness, and quiet rebellion.

Item #3: Discuss the results of sinful pride, both eternal and temporal. Talk about how God views pride.

Item #4: Explore which actions your kids think are truly prideful and which are not. Allow for some disagreement on these. See if your kids can come up with a working definition of pride.

Item #5: Have your kids share their symptoms of pride. Refer them back to the biblical examples—a haughty spirit, a boastful tongue, and an attitude of disdain. Point them also to the cure for pride—a lowly spirit, an attitude of humility, and a willingness to do without.

To Close the Session:

Explain to your group that pride puts distance between a person and God faster than anything else. Prideful people set themselves up as their own supreme authority. In other words, they become their own god. Let them know that people who have the humility to obey God are people who are blessed and rewarded by him. People who can have the humility to see others as having worth and value end up having more friends than those who think they are too cool to stain themselves with "lower class" people. Explain how Christ dissolved the barriers of pride by eating with social outcasts and picking common people for his disciples.

Outside Activity:

Have each student in your group write out one of the proverbs studied today to hang in his or her locker or room as a constant reminder of what his or her attitude should be towards God and others.

BLOWING YOUR STACK!

1 Think of the last time you lost your temper. Check the boxes below that most closely describe that situation:

I lost my temper with: ___A brother ___A sister ___A parent ___A friend ___A kid my age ___An animal ___A member of the opposite sex ___A stranger ___Other: _____

I got mad about: ___What somebody said ___I don't remember, but it was bad ___What somebody should ___What somebody did to me have done but didn't ___What somebody did to another ___Other: _____

2 What is the difference between being angry and losing your temper?

Being angry: **Losing your temper:**

3 Rate the ways people react when they lose their temper, with **1** being the worst and **8** being not so terrible. Then put checks by the behaviors *you* demonstrate when you blow your stack.

____ Slam doors and bang around
____ Scream and yell
____ Get mad at people who have nothing to do with the situation
____ Clench fists, grind teeth, bulge eyes, breathe hard
____ Say hurtful words
____ Hit, slap, scratch, push
____ Throw things, destroy property
____ Use foul language and curses

4 Do you think a temper is a controllable thing? ____Yes ____ No
Why or why not?

5 Look up the following passages and connect them to the point they make:

Proverbs 16:32	A person who gets quickly annoyed acts foolishly.
Proverbs 19:19	A gentle answer will calm down a person who is angry.
Proverbs 12:16	We should not let anger build up in us, but solve it within the day.
Proverbs 15:1	A wise person tries to work things out.
Proverbs 15:18	A person who patiently handles conflict is better than a brave soldier.
James 1:19	A person with a temper will get into trouble over and over again.
Ephesians 4:26	Listen more, speak less, and be slow to get angry.

6 Can you think of someone who you recently blew your stack at? Write that person's name here:_____
Would you be willing to go to this person and ask forgiveness for losing your cool? ___Yes ___No
Why or why not?_____

BLOWING YOUR STACK!

Topic: Controlling your temper.
Biblical Basis: Proverbs 16

Purpose of this Session:

All of us have tempers. It is not uncommon for young people to see tempers flare in hurtful ways in adults who should have long ago brought them under control. This TalkSheet will give your kids an opportunity to examine how they react to disturbing situations, and to discuss what kind of behavior and self-control they should strive for.

To Introduce the Topic:

Set up three corners of the room: One for short-fused people, one for even-tempered people, and one for very easygoing people. Suggest various temper-inducing situations, then tell kids to go to the corner that would represent how they would handle the pressure to explode in anger. Situations you can suggest include: someone insults you; someone insults your mother; someone beats up your friend; someone beats up your five-year-old brother; someone breaks something and then blames you; someone cusses you out; someone slaps around a person in a wheelchair.

The Discussion:

Item #1: Continue the dialogue you have started by discussing the last time your kids lost their tempers and why. Discuss over what and why they lost their cool. Share a situation where you lost your temper and why.
Item #2: Talk about the difference between being angry and losing your temper. Even Jesus was angry at times. Help your kids to distinguish the difference.
Item #3: Point out how much damage can be done when a person blows his or her stack. Ask your kids to share how they react when someone else blows his or her stack.
Item #4: Have kids share their answers. Ask, "Can people control their tempers, or is there a point where everyone loses their ability to control themselves?" Allow for disagreement.
Item #5: Help your kids to look into the Bible's teaching on anger. Discuss how a person can attempt to use calmness and patience to defuse a volatile situation.
Item #6: Ask your students to think carefully about how they handled their last temper tantrums. Encourage them to seek that person out and ask for forgiveness for mishandling the situation.

To Close the Session:

Remind your students that they can be justified for *feeling* anger, but can still be wrong in what they *do* with their anger. Stress the need for godly self-control in the area of anger.

Outside Activity:

Invite your kids to find a partner that they can call if a situation comes up in the next week that provokes them to anger. The job of the partner is to urge self-control, patience, and restraint, as well as being a listening ear.

and then He said...

1 If you had a secret that you wanted to tell one person, who would it be?

___Best friend   ___Parent   ___Minister   ___Teacher   ___Brother or sister

___Grandparent   ___Coach   ___Total stranger   ___Other: _____

2 Have you ever had someone tell others what you told them in confidence? ___Yes ___No

If yes, how did it make you feel? _____

How did it change your relationship with the person you told the secret to?

_____

3 For which of the "**secrets**" below would you break the confidence of a friend and tell someone else? (Circle the ones you would reveal.)

Your friend tells you who he or she is secretly in love with.

Your friend says she is pregnant.

Your friend confesses he or she cheated on the English final.

Your friend tells you something he or she is ashamed of doing.

Your friend tells you that his or her uncle is sexually abusing him or her.

Your friend tells you that he or she is experimenting with drugs.

Your friend tells you that he or she is going to run away from home.

Your friend tells you that he or she is HIV positive.

Your friend tells you that he or she is thinking of suicide.

4 Read the passages below. Pick out a short phrase that describes the idea behind each verse:

Proverbs 11:13:_____

Proverbs 17:9:_____

Proverbs 20:19:_____

Ephesians 4:29:_____

Date Used_____ Group _____

AND THEN HE SAID...

Topic: Gossip.
Biblical Basis: Proverbs 17

Purpose of this Session:

Young people often have lots of secrets. As they pull away from their parents, teens find themselves less willing to disclose private thoughts to their parents. Instead, most kids trust other kids with their secrets, often with the result of an information leak. For some kids, nothing is as fun as to leak a juicy tidbit from somebody's life. This is known in the Bible as *gossip*—the telling of what does not need to be told for the fun of the telling.

Gossip is a national pastime in our culture. Adults, kids, and the media seem to revel in gossip. But while it is fun to hear, gossip is also hurtful. It can destroy reputations and tear apart friendships. This TalkSheet will help kids to discover that only some things need to be shared with others, and that keeping a confidence will strengthen friendships and build trust between people.

To Introduce the Topic:

As your kids come into the room, start whispering about them to other students. From time to time, point and giggle. Whisper that they are to do this (whisper, laugh, and point) to other kids as they arrive. Use this as a way to begin the discussion about gossip.

Another idea is to buy an edition of a supermarket tabloid, select two or three articles, and bring them to the class with you. Ask your students to vote on which stories they think are true and which they think are false. Discuss what sells those tabloids. Rewrite one of the stories using the names of some of the kids in your group. Talk about what it would feel like to have these kind of stories written about us.

The Discussion:

Item #1: Allow your students to discuss who they would be most likely to trust with a secret. Have a few willing students share why they would trust the person they named.

Item #2: Discuss the feelings that come when a confidence has been violated. Have a few willing students share what happened to them, and what the betrayal by their friends did to their relationship.

Item #3: Go over which secrets a real friend would not keep (e.g., suicide threats, sexual abuse). Then ask kids which other secrets should be revealed. Be prepared for a lot of disagreement on some of these issues.

Item #4: Have a few willing students share their phrases (e.g., being trustworthy, betraying a confidence, promoting love, wholesome talk). Talk to your students about the impact that breaking a confidence has on friendships, trust, and our integrity as Christians.

To Close the Session:

Point out to your students that we human beings are funny creatures. We love the tidbits of scandal, the lure of knowing something that others would rather keep private. Explain that this is our old nature at work, keeping us busy with nonsense or intrigue and focused on anything but the essentials of true Christian living. Address the need to keep watch over what we say and whom we say it to.

Outside Activity:

Help your students create a pin out of old buttons and hasps (which can be purchased at most craft stores) that each of them can wear to school or churches as a reminder that they are to "Button Their Lips" when it comes to gossip. This can be real fun if all of the kids refuse to tell others what the pins stand for. It will make people crazy and may start a fad, or cause lots of gossip about the button pin itself.

A FRIEND INDEED!

1. Is it easy or hard to make friends? ____Easy ____Hard
Is it easy or hard to keep friends for a long time? ____Easy ____Hard
Is it easy or hard to break apart a friendship? ____Easy ____Hard

2. If you were able to go into a supermarket of "friends" and select qualities off the shelf that are important to a friendship, which five of the following would you pick? (Circle only five.)

Similar interests	Loyal	Funny	Smart	Athletic
Keep secrets	Musical	Popular	Truthful	Spiritual
Trustworthy	Honest	Good-looking	Same age	Same race
Wealthy	Outgoing	Christian	Creative	Humble
Easygoing	Witty	Patient	Kind	Generous
Clean	Cheerful	Courageous	Responsible	Industrious

3. Read the following Bible passages. What does each passage say about what a friend is like?
Proverbs 17:17 _____
Proverbs 18:24 _____
Proverbs 27:6 _____
Proverbs 27:9-10 _____

4. Which do you think are true or false about friendship?
a. A friend will never tell you what you don't want to hear. ___T ___F
b. A friend will stick with you no matter what. ___T ___F
c. A friend can be closer to you than a relative. ___T ___F
d. A friend will try to prevent another friend from making a bad choice. ___T ___F
e. Two friends will like the very same things. ___T ___F
f. A friendship can be worn out by too much togetherness. ___T ___F
g. A Christian would be sure to tell their friends about Christ. ___T ___F
h. A Christian should only have Christian friends. ___T ___F

5. If you were to write the words on a tombstone for your best friend, what would you say?

What would you want to be said about you by your best friends?

Best friend

Me

A FRIEND INDEED!

Topic: Friendship.
Biblical Basis: Proverbs 17; 18; 27

Purpose of this Session:

Friendships are paramount in the life of a young person. As friendships become more and more important, kids must learn what creates and sustains valuable and lasting friendships. They must learn what kind of friends to cultivate as well as what kind of friends to avoid. Most importantly, they must learn what kind of friend they need to become. This TalkSheet will help kids to discover that friends can be one of the greatest gifts that God gives them.

To Introduce the Topic:

Give your students paper and pencils. Tell them to draw four columns on their paper. In each column, have them write the following seven headings: Name; Hobbies and Interests; Color; Pets; Entertainment; Sports; Worst Moment. When you say "Go," each kid must interview four other students and get all of the information from them including their first, middle, and last names, any hobbies or interests (they must say something), their favorite colors, what pets they have or last had, their favorite movies, TV programs, or bands, any sports they enjoy, and the worst moments in their lives.

Give a prize to the first person to get all four columns completely filled. Have a few willing students read out information about others they discovered. Then talk about how friendships often develop as we discover more about each other.

The Discussion:

Item #1: Talk about the process of making and keeping friends. Discuss what might cause friendships to dissolve and what can make friendships last a long time.

Item #2: Discuss the qualities of a real friend. Explore which are the most desirable to have.

Item #3: Have a few willing students share their answers (e.g., a friend loves at all times, loyalty is important, you can trust a real friend, you don't run out on your friends). Talk about the ideas the Bible contributes to the area of friendship. Discuss why a friend who has to tell you bad news is better than flattery from an enemy, and why friends are important to have for advice and help.

Item #4: Discuss myths and fallacies about friendship. Talk about the need to have both Christian and non-Christian friends as well as our responsibility to share Christ with our nonbelieving friends.

Item #5: Have your kids share what they would say about a friend as a tribute. Discuss the things that make these friendships special.

To Close the Session:

Point out to your kids the need to *be* a friend as well as accumulate them. Let them know that friendships take work, patience, and wisdom if they are going to last. Tell them about some of the famous friendships in the Bible like David and Jonathan, Jesus and his disciples, and Paul and Timothy. Point out that we should never use our friends, but seek ways to help them out.

Outside Activity:

Ask your kids to attempt to make a new friend this week. They can do this by inviting someone they do not know well to eat lunch with them at school, bringing someone to youth group, or another simple activity.

wise up

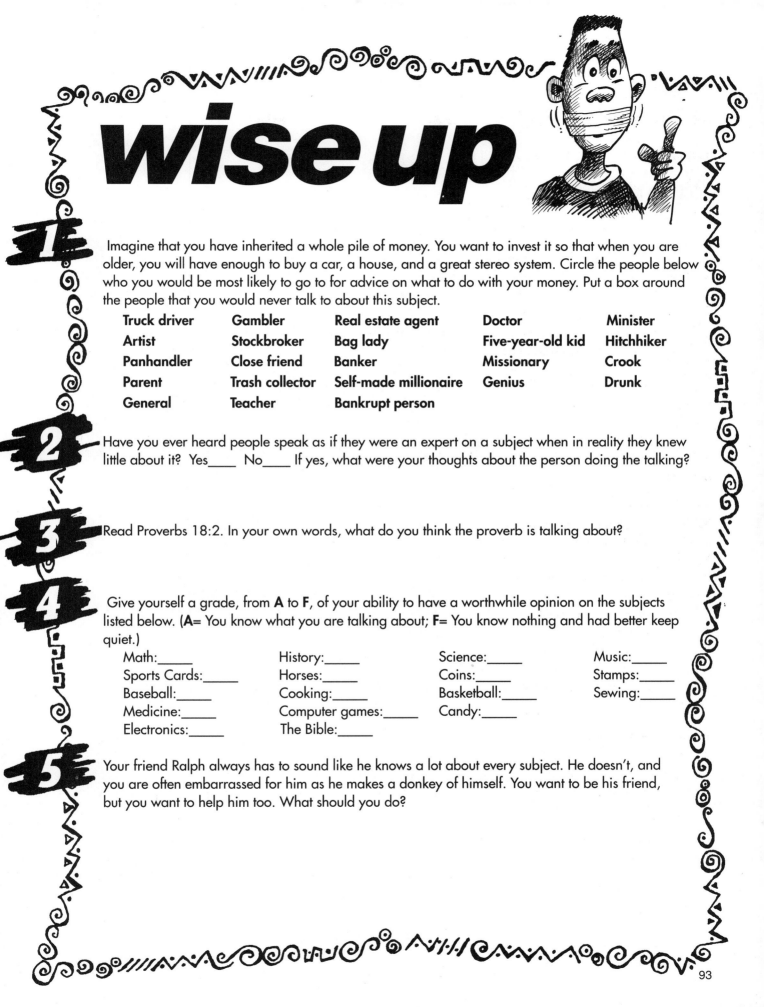

1. Imagine that you have inherited a whole pile of money. You want to invest it so that when you are older, you will have enough to buy a car, a house, and a great stereo system. Circle the people below who you would be most likely to go to for advice on what to do with your money. Put a box around the people that you would never talk to about this subject.

Truck driver	Gambler	Real estate agent	Doctor	Minister
Artist	Stockbroker	Bag lady	Five-year-old kid	Hitchhiker
Panhandler	Close friend	Banker	Missionary	Crook
Parent	Trash collector	Self-made millionaire	Genius	Drunk
General	Teacher	Bankrupt person		

2. Have you ever heard people speak as if they were an expert on a subject when in reality they knew little about it? Yes____ No____ If yes, what were your thoughts about the person doing the talking?

3. Read Proverbs 18:2. In your own words, what do you think the proverb is talking about?

4. Give yourself a grade, from **A** to **F**, of your ability to have a worthwhile opinion on the subjects listed below. (**A**= You know what you are talking about; **F**= You know nothing and had better keep quiet.)

Math:____	History:____	Science:____	Music:____
Sports Cards:____	Horses:____	Coins:____	Stamps:____
Baseball:____	Cooking:____	Basketball:____	Sewing:____
Medicine:____	Computer games:____	Candy:____	
Electronics:____	The Bible:____		

5. Your friend Ralph always has to sound like he knows a lot about every subject. He doesn't, and you are often embarrassed for him as he makes a donkey of himself. You want to be his friend, but you want to help him too. What should you do?

WISE UP

Topic: Speaking wisely.
Biblical Basis: Proverbs 18

Purpose of this Session:

Everyone has an opinion. Most people offer them willingly on subjects they know little about. Young people are no exceptions. Often they can be heard loudly stating their ideas on all kinds of things they know nothing about.

Godly wisdom teaches us to seek understanding, insight, and knowledge. It teaches us to listen more than we talk. It is good advice for an age who thinks that just because we have the ability to express our opinions, we ought to do so. This TalkSheet session will help your students see that while everyone *has* an opinion, not everyone is entitled to *hold* an opinion.

To Introduce the Topic:

Have your group stand in the center of the room. Ask all of the kids who think foreign cars are better than domestic cars go to the left, and those who disagree to the right. Then ask all those who think Ford builds better cars to go to the left side of the room, those who prefer GM to the middle, and those who consider Chrysler to be the best to go to the right. Allow those who don't have a clue to sit down. Try the same thing with different brands of cereal, different makes of clothing, etc. Talk about how many have an opinion about most everything and are quick to show it. Show that with some things (like which breakfast cereal tastes best) it doesn't matter, but with other things, our opinion may demonstrate our ignorance.

The Discussion:

Item #1: Most kids are wise enough to know the difference between those who deserve to be consulted about a money question and those who do not. Discuss why we hold better opinions of some people than others.
Item #2: Have a few willing students share their examples. Discuss what a person who talks about what he or she doesn't know is doing to his or her reputation.
Item #3: Have a few willing kids share their answers. Discuss what makes the person a fool—the lack of motivation to truly understand a situation in favor of airing one's own opinion about that situation.
Item #4: Ask your kids to share in what areas they have some degree of authority and knowledge. Talk about why a person cannot be an expert in everything. Find out how your kids graded themselves on Bible knowledge. How does that area rank on their scores?
Item #5: Talk about what to say to someone who talks about what they do not know. Discuss appropriate ways to respond when *we* are asked an opinion about something we know little or nothing about.

To Close the Session:

Remind your kids that they will often hear people talking about things they know little or nothing about. This is particularly true when it comes to the Bible. They will hear ideas and opinions about the Bible from people who have never read it. Tell them that God wants us to be people who speak wisely, who seek understanding and information rather than react blindly. He wants us to be the kind of people who know what we are talking about.

Outside Activity:

Ask each of your kids to become a mini-expert on one subject that interests them during the next week. Have a few willing students share about their new subject of interest at your next meeting.

MAKING A LOAN TO GOD

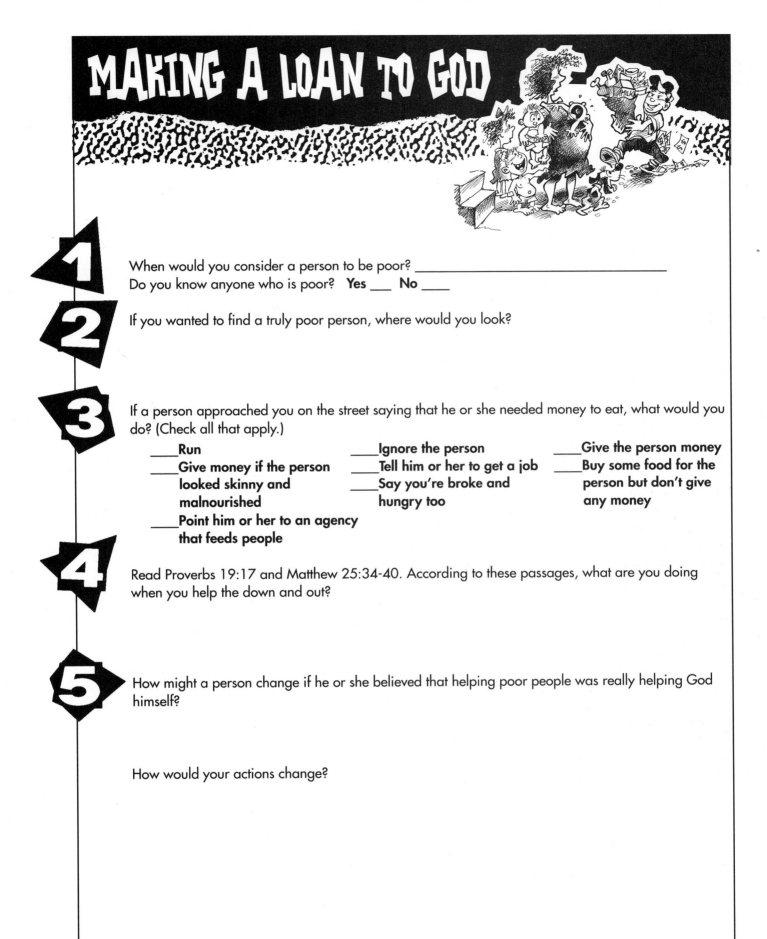

1 When would you consider a person to be poor? _____
Do you know anyone who is poor? **Yes** ___ **No** ____

2 If you wanted to find a truly poor person, where would you look?

3 If a person approached you on the street saying that he or she needed money to eat, what would you do? (Check all that apply.)

____**Run**
____**Give money if the person looked skinny and malnourished**
____**Point him or her to an agency that feeds people**

____**Ignore the person**
____**Tell him or her to get a job**
____**Say you're broke and hungry too**

____**Give the person money**
____**Buy some food for the person but don't give any money**

4 Read Proverbs 19:17 and Matthew 25:34-40. According to these passages, what are you doing when you help the down and out?

5 How might a person change if he or she believed that helping poor people was really helping God himself?

How would your actions change?

MAKING GOD A LOAN

Topic: Generosity to the poor.
Biblical Basis: Proverbs 19

Purpose of this Session:

Most kids live in an insulated world. They rarely struggle with inadequate food or shelter. They seldom give a thought to those who, through no fault of their own, must scratch mere subsistence out of tough daily toil. For most students, the poor do not exist.

This TalkSheet session is designed to heighten your students' awareness of the responsibility that Christians have to help those who suffer poverty. The Bible gives a powerful message about God's identification with those in suffering. Kids will learn that to bless the poor is to bless God.

To Introduce the Topic:

Have each of your students count the money in their pocket, purse, or wallet. Divide your group into the *Paupers* (those who have no money at all), the *Poor* (those with a dollar or less), the *Middle Class* (those with five dollars or less), and the *Rich* (those with over five dollars on them). Put the *Paupers* on the floor in the rear of the class. Give the *Poor* one chair to fight over; give the *Middle Class* one chair each. Give all the extra chairs to the *Rich* to keep, sell or give away. Do the same with any other items you might have, such as a box of cookies or sodas. Discuss how it *feels* to be poor. Talk about what the rich in the class could have done with their abundance.

The Discussion:

Item #1: Ask your students to define what it means to be poor. Does it depend on what country they live in? Are there poor living in Beverly Hills? Find out if any of them know a genuinely poor person.

Item #2: Since many kids may not know anyone who is truly poor, discuss where they might find people who are really poor—in the inner city, in countries like Mexico, perhaps in their own communities.

Item #3: Have a few willing students share their answers. Discuss the difficulties of trying to decide if the need is real or a scam. Allow for some disagreement on this point.

Item #4: Talk about the surprising idea in the Bible—kindness to the poor is seen as kindness to God himself.

Item #5: Ask kids to discuss how their actions might change towards those in poverty if they seriously thought that it was God who was getting the results of their actions. Have a few willing students share what actions they would take.

To Close the Session:

Challenge your students to commit to participate in a program that would help those who are suffering from the effects of poverty. For example, World Vision has an excellent program called the *30-Hour Famine*. They can be contacted by writing World Vision, 919 West Huntington Drive, Monrovia, CA 91016 or by calling 818-357-7979.

Outside Activities:

Take your students to serve food at a local rescue mission or do a blanket round-up for the poor people in Mexico. For example, you could sponsor a dinner for adults where the kids make the meal, and the entrance fee is a blanket per person.

PEACEMAKER

1 Which of the following would be likely to irritate you enough to get into a fight?
(Check all that apply.)

___Someone calls you foul names
___You are accused of something
    you didn't do
___Someone tries to humiliate you in public
___Someone tries to steal from you

____Someone calls your mother foul names
____You are shoved around for no reason
____Someone tries to beat up your friend
____Someone tries to steal your girlfriend or
    boyfriend

2 Rate how quickly you get into a fighting mood over an aggravating situation, with **1** being very slowly and **10** being very quickly:

VERY COOL   1   2   3   4   5   6   7   8   9   10   **LOOK OUT!**

3 Which is braver to do: __Get into a fight or argument   __Control yourself and walk away
Why?

4 Read Proverbs 20:3. What could be mottos for the fool and for the person of honor, based on this verse?

The motto for a fool would be: _____

The motto for an honorable person would be: _____

5 Match the troublesome situation with the best response (some situations may have the same response):

You are teased by a bunch of goons
You are shoved by the school bully
Your parents unfairly ground you
Someone insults you
Someone vandalizes your stuff
You are cheated by someone

Listen to their side of the story and try to discuss
Pray for them
Do nothing, just walk away
Don't show your anger, smile instead, and leave
Report to authorities
Show them kindness in spite of their deeds

6 What are the possible benefits that could result from dealing with heated situations in peaceful ways?

PEACEMAKER

Topic: Avoiding conflict.
Biblical Basis: Proverbs 20

Purpose of this Session:

Confrontations are a part of life. For a typical young teen, the potential for confrontations and quarrels is great. The solutions to conflict offered by society are often of the worst kind, emphasizing violence and vindictiveness.

In stark contrast, the Bible says that someone who quiets the potential for strife is a person of honor. The bravest action in a confrontation is always that which leads to peace. This is good news not only for kids who fear bullies, but for any kid who stumbles into a heated situation. This TalkSheet session will help your students see that peacemakers truly are blessed!

To Introduce the Topic:

On a chalkboard, write *Little weaker guy wipes out big mean guy*. Ask your kids to think of books, movies, and TV shows where this theme is prevalent. Write the titles on the board. Discuss how many of these are based on truth or fantasy. Talk about what normally happens when a little weak person goes against a big mean guy. Find out what your group thinks is the wisest thing for a little weak person to do when confronted with a big mean person.

The Discussion:

Item #1: Talk about the things that would draw your students into a quarrel or a fight. Invite the kids to offer other situations in addition to the examples on the TalkSheet.

Item #2: Have a few willing students share their ratings. Explore whether there are particular incidents that produce knee-jerk responses in many or most of your kids.

Item #3: Talk about which is the braver thing to do in a typical confrontation: to fight or to walk away. What do your kids think about this? Allow for disagreement. Discuss any exceptions that may arise.

Item #4: Explore the wisdom of the Scripture on this topic. See if your kids can reach a consensus on mottos for an honorable person and for a fighting fool. Talk about the honor that comes with being a peacemaker.

Item #5: Discuss what kind of responses would tend to calm down a potentially hostile situation. You may have some kids who strongly disagree with these resposes. Talk about the kind of courage and self-control it takes to avoid a quarrel.

Item #6: Try to help your kids understand the benefits that can come from being a person who soothes problems—staying out of trouble at school, avoiding injury, helping others to discover alternatives to violence, etc.

To Close the Session:

Ask your kids to commit Proverbs 20:3 to memory in order to always have it in mind when a confrontation arises. Have your kids pair off and say the passage to each other. Award small prizes to those who can repeat the passage from memory at your next meeting.

Outside Activity:

Ask your kids to write down on a slip of paper the name of one person that they typically have conflict with. Allow them to keep this person's name a secret. Invite students to pray for their persons every day, and to put into practice peacekeeping actions and words. Discuss any changes or progress made in these relationships during the following weeks.

GOOD REP

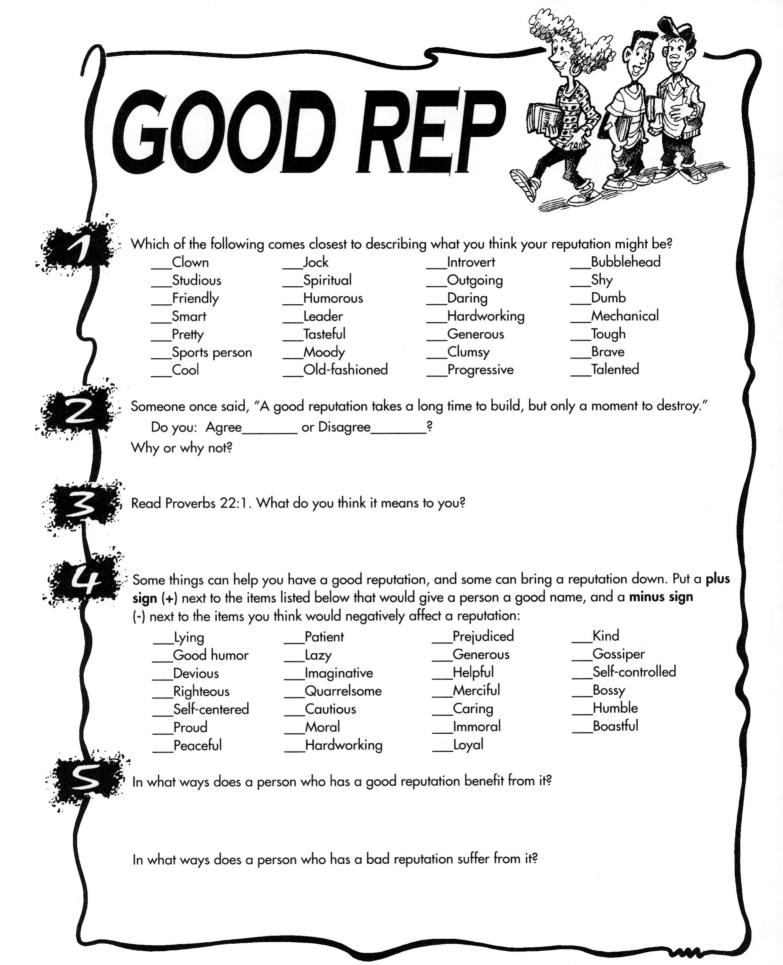

1 Which of the following comes closest to describing what you think your reputation might be?

___Clown	___Jock	___Introvert	___Bubblehead
___Studious	___Spiritual	___Outgoing	___Shy
___Friendly	___Humorous	___Daring	___Dumb
___Smart	___Leader	___Hardworking	___Mechanical
___Pretty	___Tasteful	___Generous	___Tough
___Sports person	___Moody	___Clumsy	___Brave
___Cool	___Old-fashioned	___Progressive	___Talented

2 Someone once said, "A good reputation takes a long time to build, but only a moment to destroy."

Do you: Agree_____ or Disagree_____?

Why or why not?

3 Read Proverbs 22:1. What do you think it means to you?

4 Some things can help you have a good reputation, and some can bring a reputation down. Put a **plus sign (+)** next to the items listed below that would give a person a good name, and a **minus sign (-)** next to the items you think would negatively affect a reputation:

___Lying	___Patient	___Prejudiced	___Kind
___Good humor	___Lazy	___Generous	___Gossiper
___Devious	___Imaginative	___Helpful	___Self-controlled
___Righteous	___Quarrelsome	___Merciful	___Bossy
___Self-centered	___Cautious	___Caring	___Humble
___Proud	___Moral	___Immoral	___Boastful
___Peaceful	___Hardworking	___Loyal	

5 In what ways does a person who has a good reputation benefit from it?

In what ways does a person who has a bad reputation suffer from it?

GOOD REP

Topic: Reputation.
Biblical Basis: Proverbs 22

Purpose of this Session:

Every kid wants to be liked, admired, and accepted. Kids dress for the approval of their peers, act out roles for the applause of their peers, and feel great pain when they think they are being rejected. This TalkSheet session deals with a subject that is right where most kids live every day: building a reputation that encourages others to like them.

A good reputation is valuable to any teen. It precedes them, it sets the tone in which they are viewed, and often predetermines the amount of trust and openness they will receive from others. Your students will learn that developing a good reputation takes effort and struggle. But it is worth it.

To Introduce the Topic:

Bring in some newspapers or magazines. Toss them to the group, along with a few pairs of scissors. Ask your kids to cut out advertisements that tie in a product with a person's reputation. Pin what they have cut out on a corkboard. Discuss why reputation would be important to consumers. Remind your kids that people are only as trustworthy as their reputations.

The Discussion:

Item #1: Have your kids select words that might describe the reputation that they think they have with others. After they have selected, have a few willing students share their answers.
Item #2: Discuss the process of building or dismantling a reputation. Share a time when your reputation suffered, what caused the problem, and what it took to repair your reputation.
Item #3: Talk about the value that the Bible applies to a good name or reputation. Ask how much the price tag would be if a person had to "buy" a good reputation.
Item #4: Explore the various characteristics or habits that would enhance or destroy a reputation. Note that the things that build a good reputation also fit with godly living.
Item #5: Have a few willing students share their answers. Try to help your kids realize the benefits of a good reputation: being trusted, being someone others come to for help and advice, gaining the respect of peers, etc.

To Close the Session:

Explain to your group that it is important that we put energy and effort into living lives that will give us a good reputation. Talk about how obeying God will produce a life that a person can be proud of. Ask your students to consider the kind of reputation that they are after, and whether that reputation will end up hurting them in the end. Close by asking your kids to contribute one thought or idea that would be a plus in building a good reputation; for example, "If you want a good name, hang around with good people."

Outside Activity:

Invite each student to select a nickname for a trait that they would like to make part of their personality and reputation. This should be a trait that they desire, but feel they have little of. The names could be out of a name book or simply made up. For example, a person who wants to listen more than they talk can take the nickname "Ears" or "Zipper Mouth." Have your students share their nicknames and commit to addressing one another by their new nicknames for the following week.

DOLLARS WITH WINGS

1 If you had three wishes that could come true, would one of them be to have lots of money?

_____Naturally _____I don't think so _____I dunno!

2 What is the largest amount of your own money you have ever spent at one time? _____
What did you spend it on? _____ Would you do it again?_____
Why or why not?_____

3 What do you think is the biggest danger in desiring to make lots of money? List them in order, with the greatest danger being number **1**, and the least danger being number **6**:

___ **Doing dishonest things to get it**
___ **Ignoring other priorities to make money**
___ **Worshipping money more than God**
___ **Thinking you don't need to depend on God anymore**
___ **Getting lots of money but no happiness**
___ **Using people for what you could get from them rather than caring
about them for who they are**

4 Read Proverbs 23:4-5. Draw a picture in the space below of what you feel this passage is talking about:

Now read about the rich man in Luke 12:15-21. Fill in the blanks to the passage below:

Jesus said to be on guard against all kinds of _____ and that a person's life does not consist in the abundance of _____. In his parable, he told of a rich man whose_____ produced a huge crop. His problem was that he didn't have enough _____for his crop. He decided to build bigger_____ and to "take life easy: _____, _____ and be _____". But God had a different idea. He said to him, "This very night your_____will be demanded from you."

God even called him a _____. Jesus commented that this is how it will be for anyone who is not _____ toward God.

5 What do these two passages tell you about the desire to get rich?

6 Where is the desire to make lots of money on your scale of important things? Mark your answer below:

*Highest priority*_____*Lowest priority*

DOLLARS WITH WINGS

Topic: The desire for wealth.
Biblical Basis: Proverbs 23

Purpose of this Session:

Most kids have little money. But that doesn't mean that they haven't discovered the power of it! Many kids have bought into the idea that happiness and money are directly related. Some of your kids may already be forming the habits and worldview that will cause them misery throughout their adult lives as they chase for the elusive pot of gold.

The Bible is cold to the topic of striving for wealth. It warns kids and adults alike that the minute they fix their gaze upon the dollar, it sprouts wings and flies away like an elusive butterfly. This TalkSheet session is designed to help your kids to see that material gain is the wrong place to put their focus, and that real eternal treasure is made up of things that don't disappear.

To Introduce the Topic:

Divide your room into two sections. Mark one section with a sign that says, "The Pay is Great;" the other section, with a sign that says, "The Work is Enjoyable." Tell your students that they must choose a career. One job pays $100,000 per year but is really boring. The other job is really fun, but pays barely enough to get by. Ask your students to select the job they would choose for a career, and to go to the sign that reflects their choice. After they have chosen, discuss the reasons for their choices. Use this discussion as an opportunity to introduce today's topic.

The Discussion:

Item #1: Use this question to further the discussion of our desire for money. Ask, "Why does money appear on so many of our wish lists?"

Item #2: Have a few willing students share their answers. See if any of your kids have regrets about money they have spent in the past. Talk about the tendency to burn with desire for some object, only to become bored with it once we have acquired it.

Item #3: Talk about the problems that money creates in our spiritual lives. See which difficulties seem most dangerous to your students. Also, find out if some kids see no danger to acquiring money. Allow for disagreement.

Item #4: Help your kids to create images that illustrate the illusory nature of wealth, especially those students who are not artists. Encourage a few kids to share their drawings, and affirm them profusely.

Item #5: Talk about where the priorities and desires of Christians should be focused. Discuss how a person builds up treasures in heaven.

Item #6: Allow your students to determine where the desire to get money sits on their priority list. See if your students can come up with a place on the graph where warning lights should go on.

To Close the Session:

Since the desire to surround ourselves with things and the urge to grasp after money is so universal, we must keep constantly on guard that we do not come under its spell. Encourage your students to make it the goal of their lives to invest in things that cannot be taken away from them.

Outside Activity:

Challenge your students to do something for a person in your church who does not have the means to repay the deed. Your kids could wash cars, mow lawns, make meals, watch the kids of weary or sick parents, etc.

A REAL LIFESAVER

1   Would you risk your life to save:
   A baby   ___Yes ___No
   An old person   ___Yes ___No
   A criminal   ___Yes ___No
   A dog   ___Yes ___No
   A friend   ___Yes ___No

2   Do you agree or disagree with the following statement: "People who need spiritual help should be responded to with the same urgency as people who need physical help."

   Agree_____   **Disagree_____**

   Why or why not?

3   Read Proverbs 24:11-12. Then, answer the following questions:
   Who is this passage directed to? _____
   Who is it talking about? _____
   What is their problem? _____
   What should we do about it? _____
   How might we try to avoid our responsibility? _____
   How could our actions be judged? _____

4   How might a person be led to spiritual death? Who might be leading them? What activities might contribute towards a person's spiritual destruction?

   _____
   _____
   _____

5   Suppose you wanted to try and rescue some of your friends from dying spiritually. List, in order of effectiveness, which ways would be the best to conduct the rescue, with number **1** being the most effective:

   ___Mail them a letter about Christ   ___Bring them to a church service   ___Give them a Bible
   ___Send the minister over   ___Act spiritual around them   ___Give them a tract
      to talk to them   ___Preach a sermon to them   ___Tell them what Christ
   ___Pray for them   ___Loan them a Christian CD   means to you
   ___Bring them to youth group

6   What are some excuses that kids might come up with for not trying to rescue their friends from a sure spiritual death?

A REAL LIFESAVER

Topic: Sharing Christ.
Biblical Basis: Proverbs 24

Purpose of this Session:

The commission to tell others the good news of Jesus Christ has no age boundaries. Young teens rub shoulders daily with those who are being led away to spiritual death by a river of false ideas flowing from a secular world. Christians are called to the rescue. Because of their proximity, kids have the initial responsibility to rescue other kids. They are closest to the scene and are trusted by their friends.

The obligation to gently but boldly share Christ with their friends is scary to most kids. They have a million reasons why they can't do it. Often this is because they think that they must give a well-defined doctrinal presentation.

This TalkSheet session is designed to not only prod kids to consider reaching out to their non-Christian friends, but to let them know that there is an effective and easy way to do it: Share about what Jesus Christ means to them personally, in their own words, and their own ways.

To Introduce the Topic:

Invite any students to talk about a recent accident they might have seen or driven by. Talk about what happened. Who was first at the scene? What actions did they take? What was the response of other bystanders? Discuss what, if anything, the kid telling the story did to help. Talk about what might have happened if there was no one around when this accident took place. Use this as an opportunity to present the idea that people can be in dire need, and that even kids can do something to help.

The Discussion:

Item #1: Have kids share who they might be motivated to risk their life to save. Many kids will likely identify a friend as one of those people. Point out that most people would risk a lot to save one of their friends.
Item #2: Allow for some disagreement here. Help your kids to define what *spiritual needs* are—that kids' very souls are in jeopardy without God.
Item #3: Be prepared for some strong reactions to this passage. It will be hard for some kids to face their responsibilities. Also, some kids will dispute that people really end up in hell.
Item #4: Help kids to understand how the everyday, unhealthy activities that any of us can fall into—obsession with money, sexual temptation, etc.—can actually lead to spiritual death.
Item #5: Discuss which method of telling others about Christ is the most effective. Let your kids brainstorm on this. Ask your students what would have the most effect upon *them*?
Item #6: Have a few willing students share their answers. Help kids to see that it's usually our *fear* that keeps us from reaching out to our friends. Point out that they don't have to be theological experts; they just have to share what God has done for them, in their own words.

To Close the Session:

Explain to your group that though it can be hard to understand, many people are in danger of being led to eternal death. Read Ephesians 2:1-5; point out that spiritual death is the result of not knowing Christ personally.

Outside Activity:

Challenge your kids to think of at least one person that they will attempt to share Christ with in some way during the next week. Have them report on the results of their efforts at your next meeting.